Why Must There Be Dragons?

Empowering Women to Master their Careers *Without* Changing Men

[handwritten inscription:] Sept 12 2008 Sarah— Thank you for your friendship & invaluable help w/ gender strategy! and Ast. Marie Royce 1 AFA

by
Trent M. Kittleman

Contributing editors
Joan Athen & Marie Royce

Why Must There Be Dragons? Empowering Women to Master their Careers Without Changing Men
By Trent M. Kittleman
Contributing editors: Joan Athen & Marie Royce

Published by:
GenderStrategy

Cover Art by:
Mike Ray
Ink Tycoon
www.InkTycoon.com

IBSN: 1438213638

Printed in the United States of America

For more information, go to **www.GenderStrategy.com**

It is the 31st Century
Earth is Different.

Human Beings were banished from the Earth in
the 25th Century
For many good and sound reasons.
Leaving behind chaos

And Chaos reigned for many years
Until at last a new Master of the Earth was
chosen

And Dog came forth to rule over all the birds of the
air
and over all the fish in the sea
and over all the other beasts of the field
. . .except for Cat.

Dog said, "Woof!"
And Cat heard, "You are all wise and knowing"

Cat replied, "Meow!"
And Dog heard, "I am your obedient servant"

That pretty much says it all . . . . .

This story is dedicated

To all of the Cats and all of the Dogs

Who work together every day

And who wonder

Why it is that Cats must be so. . .

so *Fe*line

And why it is that Dogs must be so . . .

so *Ca*nine

CONTENTS

APPENDICES

Introduction

Any woman who has been in the workforce for any length of time has seen younger, 'less talented' men get the choice assignments and the promotions and has thought: it <u>must</u> be discrimination.

Sometimes it is.

But sometimes it isn't.

This book is about **what it is** when it isn't discrimination. Because *then* you can fix it.

WHY MUST THERE BE DRAGONS? is a fable set in the 31st century, where dogs and cats run the world. The canines and felines are metaphors for men and women and exhibit traits that are eerily similar to those of their human counterparts.

The protagonist of the book, Kathryn ("Kat") Wu, does not pretend that the workplace is equal or easy. Nor does she suggest changing the workplace or the canines who run it. Systemic changes are best left to time, CFR departments and committed CEOs. Kat accepts the workplace as it is and seeks to help both canines and felines work more effectively together.

The book is divided into three sections. Part 1 sets the stage by introducing us to the fictitious company, Feline Foods, its major players, and its 'feline integration' problem.

Parts 2-5 begin with Kat and her corporate side-kick, Ryan ("Wolfe") Wolfhound holding a set of interviews. The first interview in each part is with a frustrated feline employee who tells her story. In the second interview, you hear the same story from her supervisors' perspective. Kat & Wolfe then discuss why the feline and canine experience such different—but equally valid—perceptions of the same set of 'facts.'

They also discuss Kat's approach to improving communication between the two species. As Kat explains to Wolfe, her approach is two-fold. First, she *educates both canines and felines* how their respective styles and patterns of communication tend to differ, and how these differences can cause miscommunications and misperceptions in the workplace. Then, she *trains felines* how to use their feline flexibility to avoid the styles and patterns of communication that create a negative perception among canines, and to focus more effort on *managing their careers.* Each of these four Parts concludes with "Lessons" for the frustrated feline (and the reader).

Part 6 concludes the lessons and finishes by explaining *why there are Dragons.*

About the Author and Contributing Editors

Joan Athen, Marie Royce, and I separately travelled long and unique career paths before coming together to form **GENDERSTRATEGY** *to empower women to manage their careers <u>without</u> changing men*. Collectively, the three of us have almost 100 years of workplace experience to draw from ranging from school bus driver (we won't say who) to CEO of a multi-billion dollar public toll agency.

Joan Athen is an entrepreneur. For more than 20 years, she developed and ran increasingly complex telecommunications companies. After selling her last business, she was sought out, offered, and accepted a Presidential appointment to head the Community College division of the U.S. Department of Education. Joan has been honored on numerous occasions for her volunteer community leadership and for her entrepreneurial and academic endeavors.

Marie Royce obtained an MBA from Georgetown University and has pursued a successful corporate career in sales and marketing. She began at Procter & Gamble, became Vice President of Choice Hotels, then Senior Director of Sales & Marketing with Marriott International, and is currently Managing Director of Global Strategic Initiatives for Alcatel-Lucent. She has also been a full-time faculty member at California State Poly-technic University, Pomona.

I began my career as a retail furniture store manager while still a single mom. Exhausted by the 363-days-a-year work schedule, I became a lawyer went to work for a large law firm. I realized I hadn't lessened my workload when the "billing" requirement exceeded 2,000 hours a year. So I sought refuge "in-house" as a corporate attorney with Marriott International. After three years, they learned of my political proclivities and transferred me to Vice President of Legislative Affairs, where golf became a major responsibility. My next career began when the new Governor of Maryland decided to appoint me Deputy Secretary of Transportation (go figure?!) and I was lured away by the potential for riches beyond imagining. Unfortunately, I had no talent for graft, so my income was modest—but the job was fun. Apparently, I did okay because after two years, he asked me to take over as President and CEO of the Maryland Transportation Authority, a multi-billion dollar toll authority with over 1,600 employees (including a *police force*). All he asked was that I eliminate the congestion on the Chesapeake Bay Bridge during the summer rush hours . . .

Clearly, we are all driven by a challenge!

The idea for his book was developed collaboratively by the three partners of GenderStrategy. The writing is mine, and I accept full responsibility for any and all errors.

-Trent Kittleman

Why Must There Be Dragons?

Part 1:

'DisCatination' at Feline Foods

"The temptation is to see the cause of the glass ceiling as 'sexism,' and surely there is truth in this characterization. But 'sexism' tells us where we are without telling us how we got there, and without providing help in getting out."

Found in the Historical Files, from the Ancient Year, 1994
<u>Talking from 9 to 5</u>, Deborah Tannen

Bernie's Bad Day

Bernard C. Rottweiler leaned back in his big executive chair, clasped his paws behind his massive head, and smiled. Bernard – or Bernie, as he liked to be called-- was the President and CEO of Feline Foods, Inc. At age 63 (9, in people years) he looked much younger, partly because he genuinely enjoyed running the huge SPCA 500 company.

Today, Bernie was basking in the memory of how his VP of Premium Brand Sales had virtually saved the company last month. He'd defeated *Regulation G* just as it was about to devour a $13 million sale. Yes, Dwight Knight really was this company's white knight and dragon-slayer. Bernie chuckled at his clever metaphor . . . or was it a simile. Oh, who cares.

Today, even the annoying memo from Wolfe couldn't sour his mood. Okay, so they were having some issues promoting felines. He'd see to it that the problem, whatever it was, got fixed. Bernie kind of liked having cats in the workplace. Feline Foods had been among the first to comply when the nation's Great Diversity Debate resulted in the "Feline Integration Project," mandating the "fair and equal treatment" of felines.   Under his leadership, Feline Foods had recruited, trained and promoted a substantial number of cats into all areas of the business.

Despite Bernie's initial misgivings about the program (who ever heard of canines and felines working side by side), things had gone surprisingly well. Sales were up, and profits had been rising steadily. In fact, profits had been steadily increasing over the exact same period of time during which the Company began seriously integrating felines into upper management. Bernie didn't necessarily believe the increase in profits was related to the increase in felines, but research at other companies showed a similar trend.

Even the Board of Directors was happy – right up until that moment.

Things started going badly at exactly 9:53 that morning. That was when the Company's CFO knocked on Bernie's big oak door.

"Bad news, Bernie," said Alan Greendog, as he walked in without waiting for permission. "My top feline accounticat just submitted her resignation."

"Why?" asked Bernie, his good mood beginning to evaporate.

"I don't really know," replied Alan. "All I know is that she's taking a job with one of our competitors. I asked Hyrum to see if he could find out why she's leaving, and he mumbled something about feline issues. Listen, I've got to get back to a meeting, but I thought you should know about this."

"I'll try and talk with her," said Bernie as Alan left. Before Bernie could pick up the phone, however, Oliver Wendell Hounds, Feline Foods Associate General Counsel for Litigation, strode into his office and dropped a thick legal document on his desk.

"What's this?" asked Bernie.

Oliver grimaced. "It's a letter-petition from some of your feline employees. I thought you might want to look it over before Leona Leopard calls."

Leona Leopard was the one and only feline on the Board of Directors, and despite her name she was a *tiger* when it came to protecting the company.

"Why would Leona be calling me?" asked Bernie in alarm. "What does she know about this? And how can she know about something like this before I do?"

At that moment, Martha Higgins, Bernie's secretary of 23 years, stuck her head in the door. "I'm sorry to interrupt, Mr. 'B,' but Director Leopard is on the phone. She said it's urgent that she talk with you. What shall I tell her?"

Bernie looked at Oliver for an explanation. "What the heck is going on, Ollie?"

"It's the cats, Bernie. A group of felines in the Company have some potentially serious complaints. . . . there's an implication that if the issues aren't resolved, they may file suit for discrimination—specifically, for *discatination*." Oliver looked at the telephone blinking persistently on Bernie's desk. "I think one of the felines is Leona Leopard's cousin. . ."

It took almost an hour for Bernie to calm Leona, which he accomplished only by promising to resolve the concerns of his feline employees before the next Board meeting. As soon as he hung up, Martha came in with the morning mail.

Hoping for a respite from the events of the past two hours, Bernie reached for the pile and said what he'd been saying for the last 15 years: "Any good news, Martha?"

At this point, Martha was supposed to say, "Not unless there's news of my raise, Mr. B!"

But Martha said nothing, and Bernie knew his morning mail was about to bring him more bad news.

It was the envelope right on top: a piece of official correspondence from the E.I.E.I.O—the Employment Institute for Engendering Increased Opportunities. Letters from the E.I.E.I.O. never brought good news, and this was no exception. It was a notice of the E.I.E.I.O's intent to perform a compliance review of Feline Foods efforts with respect to the Feline Integration Project. Although the notice said that the selection of Feline Foods had been "random," Bernie knew that random compliance reviews were about as likely as "random" IRS audits.

Bernie let his massive head sink onto his huge forepaws. He wasn't sure how so much had gone so wrong in so short a time, but it had. Eventually, he raised his head and snatched up the letter-petition Oliver left him and began to read. The authors of the complaint were some of the higher-ranked cats in the Company, which surprised him.   Their primary complaint seemed to be lack of high-profile opportunities and being passed over for promotion.   As Bernie turned to the last page of the letter-petition, he saw the Company Letterhead and recognized the document as a copy of a memorandum he'd recently received from his Executive VP, Ryan ("Wolfe") Wolfhound—a *confidential* memorandum.

Blast it!   How had they gotten a copy of that memorandum?! Nonetheless, it was clear from the letter-petition that the memo was just confirmation of what the cats already believed. Apparently, there was an undercurrent of feline unrest well before the executives even met to consider promotions. What really pissed Bernie off, however, was that he should have known about this unrest *weeks* ago. He really

Feline Foods
The finest feline feast in the East

HIGHLY CONFIDENTIAL – FOR YOUR EYES ONLY

To: Bernard Rottweiler, President & CEO
From: Ryan Wolfhound, Executive VP, Special Projects
Date: January 29, 3003
Re: Promotions

Bernie:

We may have a problem. Last week, I met with the executive vice presidents to come up with the annual promotion recommendations. This year, there were 85 candidates in the pool. Attached is the list of the top 20, based on our evaluations.

Before you figure it out for yourself, there are no cats on the list. Almost half the names we reviewed were cats, and we discussed every candidate thoroughly. But the same concern kept coming up -- 'She lacks confidence.'

We know you want us to promote cats, but not one of your EVP's wanted to promote someone who couldn't do the job. Like the EVP of Sales and Marketing said, "How's my sales staff going to react to someone who says, 'well, I *think* my new sales pitch will sell more Premium Plus. . . but I'm not sure'!"

Let me know how you want me to handle this.

Wolfe

hated being caught flat-pawed.   This is Hyrum's fault, thought Bernie.

"Martha!" Bernie bellowed, "Get that little twerp from CFR up here to see me—NOW!"

The unfortunate "little twerp from CFR" was Feline Foods' Director of CFR (Canine/Feline Resources), Hyrum N. Fyrum.

When Hyrum arrived breathless and red-faced a short time later, Bernie greeted him with ill-concealed hostility.

"If it wouldn't be too much of an imposition, would you mind explaining what happened to our progress on the Feline Integration Project?"   Hyrum winced at the scathing tone, but before he could respond, Bernie continued.

"Is there some reason you haven't bothered to tell me that the sum total of our efforts on the Feline Integration Project has been to hire a whole herd of cats into positions from which they apparently cannot be promoted?   And did you plan to let me know anytime soon that half the Company's employees are busy drafting lawsuits against us?   I realize it may not be particularly important to *you* that I'm getting angry calls from the Board of Directors who seem to know more about what's going on in my Company than *I* do, but indulge me—give me a *hint* as to what you plan to do about all this! And do you think it will be any time before *the E.I.E.I.O. shuts us down?"*

After 20 years, Hyrum was used to this kind of abuse. Despite his diminutive size (Hyrum was a Yorkshire terrier) Hyrum was not bothered by Bernie's tantrums.

"Well, Bernie," he began, adjusting his legendary red bow tie and clearing his voice. "I believe I've found the source of the problem.   You see, the department heads—who are almost all canines—they rate their feline employees very highly. Every one of them that I spoke with had nothing but praise for their feline managers, as far as doing a good job . . . which *should* lead to a promotion, wouldn't you think? And certainly, that's what the *cats* thought . . . er, think. But when it comes to *leadership* skills, it seems the cats don't display the kind of confidence—the 'confident demeanor'—that their bosses are looking for in a leader. Of course, none of the felines believe this . . .so. . . so you see, when they aren't promoted . . . well, the only explanation left to them is . . . well . . . systemic discatination." Hyrum finished.

"How can they THINK that!?!" bellowed Bernie with real anger and frustration. "It's infuriating! I've done everything caninely possible to ensure that we have cats in every conceivable kind of job in this Company. I've personally recruited two of the finest accounticats in the nation. Our Company's Deputy General Counsel is a cat, for heaven's sake. How can they . . . who is it. . . who says that I. . ."

"Calm down, Bernie," said Hyrum. "It isn't *you*. It just seems that most of the felines feel that they don't get a fair shot at the top jobs. Unfortunately, the numbers seem to support this conclusion."

"So tell me, Mr. Executive Vice President of Canine-Feline Resources, how are you going to FIX IT?"

"I do have a suggestion," said Hyrum tentatively.

"Well, well!" said Bernie grinning dangerously. "Do you suppose I could persuade you to TELL ME your suggestion?"

"Actually, Bernie," said Hyrum, smiling for the first time. "I think I'd rather introduce you."

"...there are some differences between [dogs] and [cats] in the workplace. Work to understand rather than deny those differences and then responsibly use that knowledge to great effect for you and your organization."

Found in the Historical Files, from the Year 2006
Helene Lerner, <u>Smart Women Take Risks</u>

K AT ON BOARD

The next morning, Hyrum entered Bernie's outer office, accompanied by an attractive feline. Martha Higgins looked up from her desk.

"Good morning, Martha," said Hyrum genially.

"Well, it's definitely morning," replied Martha, dourly.

"Oh come now, Martha. It's too early to be that grumpy," teased Hyrum.

"Yes, but Mr. 'B' has *been here* all morning!"

"Oh, well, that explains it!" said Hyrum, studiously ignoring Bernie, who had come out of his office during this exchange and who was now glowering playfully down at Martha.

"Tell me again why I don't fire you," he growled at his long-suffering secretary.

"Because without me, you couldn't find your tail using all four paws!" said Martha. "Now get back into your office and talk to Hyrum and this nice feline, Ms. . . . (Martha peered at the schedule on her desk) . . . Ms. Woo, I believe it is."   Martha rose and ushered them into Bernie's office, shutting the door behind them.

Inside the office, Hyrum straightened his red bow tie reflexively and began. "Bernie, this is Kathryn Woo, the feline consultant I told you about."

"It's 'Kat', and it's a pleasure to meet you, Mr. Rottweiler," said Kat, extending her elegant paw. Her sleek coat shimmered under the slanted rays of the morning sun streaking through the panoramic windows. The regal bearing of her Siamese heritage was evident in the arch of her back, the sculptured face, and the pointed ears. The steady gaze of her cobalt blue eyes completed the impression of competence that she exuded like fine perfume. Bernie liked what he saw.

"The pleasure is mine, Ms. Woo -- Kat," said Bernie. "So, tell me about yourself. I understand that you were a CFR executive at Compu-Cat Research & Technology for over 10 years."

"That's right.," said Kat. "I was their Director of Canine/Feline Resources in charge of training."

"Hyrum speaks very highly of you. Tell me, why did you leave Compu-Cat?"

"About six months ago, my boss, Gary Golden, retired, and Compu-Cat brought in a new Vice President of CFR from the outside – a Doberman named Heinrich Hammer. Mr. Hammer had a totally different agenda than my old boss. Heinrich felt that training employees was far less important to the Company than hiring the right employees to begin with."

"That's an arguable position," said Bernie.

"I know that hiring the right employee is important," agreed Kat. "But Heinrich wanted to scrap virtually all of our training programs and spend all of those funds in advertising on *Monster.com* or *CareerBuilder.com*; he was enthralled with those Internet recruiting sites."

"You didn't agree with his approach?" asked Hyrum.

"No, I didn't. What good does it do to recruit the best employees if you can't keep them? Of course, I had a personal interest in the Company's training because I developed most of the feline training courses. But more importantly, they were working. Last year, the number of felines promoted into management doubled. This didn't happen through 'quotas.' It happened because these cats understood what their bosses were looking for, and they were able to exhibit the leadership necessary to get those jobs."

"Did you explain all this to Hammer?" asked Bernie.

"I did. But he was committed to a new way of doing things."

Bernie smiled inwardly at the tactful way Kat phrased that response. "So you left?"

"Yes. I knew I couldn't stay and give Heinrich my full support when his first act was to dismantle the programs I'd spent years designing and implementing. And he was the boss," Kat concluded.

"I see," said Bernie, "So what have you been doing since you left?"

"I started my own management training firm," said Kat with a smile. "Fortunately, I've had as much work as I can handle."

"Well," said Bernie turning to Hyrum, "I suppose you think that Ms. Woo can help us?"

"I do, Bernie, I do," said Hyrum. "Gary Golden was my counterpart at Compu-Cat for the last ten years. He just raved about the impact Kat's training had on his employees – both canine and feline."

"How much will all of this cost us?" asked Bernie.

"A whole lot less than a lawsuit," Hyrum mumbled.

Bernie glared at Hyrum, and Kat took advantage of the momentary silence.

"Let me tell you how I work, Bernie. For a company this size, I like to analyze the needs and customize my program. I charge a flat fee for the analysis, which generally takes a week or two. But it requires your help. I'll need access to your employees and one of your key executives to work with. At the end of the period, I'll write up a report and proposal. You can review my report, talk with your executive, and make the decision then as to whether you want to hire me. You get to keep the report, the proposal, and all of my work product for the two-week period regardless of your decision. Does that sound fair?"

More than fair, Bernie thought.

"All right, Ms. Woo. You've got yourself a deal," said Bernie. Looking at Hyrum, he continued. "You'll talk with Ms. Woo and make the necessary arrangements, Hyrum?"

"Yes, yes, I will, Bernie. Indeed, we have already begun discussions," said Hyrum. As Bernie rose to end the meeting, Hyrum continued quickly. "About the executive Kat needs? I thought Wolfe would be a good choice. He's still recovering from knee surgery, and this might be a good way for him to ease back into work..."

"Why can't someone from your department do it, Hyrum," said Bernie.

Kat answered. "If you want your executive team to pay attention, Bernie, support for my efforts has to come from the top."

Bernie didn't like the idea of sacrificing the services of one of his top executives. But Hyrum's suggestion of Wolfe made sense. . . . In fact, it might just be good for Wolfe, thought Bernie with a chuckle.

"Okay. You can have Wolfe for the two weeks. . . .if you can put up with him that long."

Kat looked askance at Hyrum.

"Pay him no mind, Kat. Wolfe is the Executive Vice President of Special Projects—Bernie's 'right-hand-man' as they say. He is perfect for what you need."

Bernie was still looking amused when he said to Kat, "Come by my office tomorrow morning and you can meet Wolfe. I'll introduce you."

"I'll be there," said Kat.

> "If supervisors learn to perceive outstanding performance regardless of the performer's style, it will be less necessary for individuals to learn to display their talents. On that happy day, the glass ceiling will become a looking glass through which a fair percentage of Alices will be able to step."
>
> *Found in the Historical files, from the Year 1980*
> *Deborah Tannen, Talking from 9 to 5*

KAT & WOLFE

The next morning, Bernie greeted Kat genially. "Kat! I'd like you to meet Ryan Wolfhound. Wolfe, this is Kat."

Wolfe growled a surly 'good morning' but did not come forward to touch paws. Kat echoed a polite good morning and studied the sullen-looking Irish wolfhound with interest. The knee of his left hind leg was wrapped in hospital-white bandages and he leaned heavily on an old-fashioned wooden crutch. But it wasn't the knee injury causing the pained expression on his handsome face – Kat was sure of that. Clearly, Wolfe was not happy with this assignment.

"What I've told Wolfe," continued Bernie, "is that you're here for two weeks to do an assessment of the problem that's preventing felines from being promoted and to provide me with a proposal for fixing it. His job is to work with you and give me his assessment. I think that about covers it. Do either of you have any questions?"

Wolfe looked at Kat. "Just how do you propose to make these cats 'promotable'?" he asked with ill-concealed sarcasm. "Magic?"

Kat bit her tongue and thought carefully about how to handle this obvious challenge. Her natural instinct was to jump down his throat at this snide insult not only to her but to all cats. But that wouldn't accomplish anything except to further alienate Wolfe, and possibly Bernie. Trying to give a rational answer to an irrational remark wouldn't do much good, either. Ultimately, she elected to reply in kind.

"You seem skeptical, Wolfe," Kat smiled. "If you think about it, you'll realize that my species has been working 'magic' for centuries. Even during the age when we had human masters, cats trained humans to tend us, feed us, and accord us all the care and luxury we desired. We'd sleep all day while your species was forced hunt foxes you weren't allowed to catch, retrieve birds you weren't allowed to eat, and play fetch at the whim of your masters. Do you really think we cats can't figure out how to manipulate canines in a workplace setting, once we set our minds to it?"

Apparently, Kat's gentle brand of sarcasm was the right approach. Wolfe's face struggled to remain hostile, but failed. The grin straining at his lips broke through into a genuine smile. Bernie, meanwhile, laughed aloud.

"Are you sure you want to let her loose around here?" Wolfe asked Bernie, tongue-in-cheek. "None of our jobs may be safe!"

"I'm willing to take my chances," said Bernie, grinning. "Now, both of you, get out of my office and let me get back to work."

As Wolfe and Kat made their way to the elevator, Kat turned serious.

"Wolfe, I really do need your help if we're going to be successful."

"Just tell me what you need," he replied, in a much better frame of mind at this point.

"Great," she said. "We need to interview at least four felines who are viewed as having strong skills, but who have encountered some kind of obstacle in their career path. I need you to identify these cats and have your secretary set up one-hour appointments with each of them – one a day. Try to select felines in all stages of their careers, if possible. And following each appointment with the cat, we need to interview her supervisor – or the executive who makes the promotion decisions, if that's someone different."

"That may take some time," Wolfe replied, mildly irritated. He was not used to taking orders from anyone other than Bernie.

"We don't have a lot of time, Wolfe. I really need to have those appointments scheduled for next week," she replied, without thinking. Immediately, she recognized her mistake. She saw from his expression that Wolfe was not reacting well to this *very direct* communication style.

Kat had momentarily forgotten the 'rules of the game.' Communicating with canines was her business and she knew she needed to adapt her style immediately, if she wanted to get and keep Wolfe's cooperation.

She lowered her voice, looked up at Wolfe and spoke gently, "I know it's not going to be easy, Wolfe – but that's why Bernie picked you to help me. You're the only one with enough respect and authority to make this effort happen quickly – or make it happen at all."

"Okay, okay," Wolfe grumbled, recognizing the flattery, but succumbing to it nonetheless. "I'll see what I can do."

"Thanks, Wolfe," said Kat.

Kat took a deep breath of relief as she slowly rode down in the elevator. She played the game well. But . . . sometimes . . . she just *hated* the damn game.

"Tact is the ability to describe others as they see themselves."

--*Abraham Lincoln*
Found in the Historical Files, from the Ancient Years

Part 2:

Learn the Rules

"I want to let you [cats] in on a secret I've learned through my years in the corporate world: There is a set of unwritten rules in business and, while you may not choose to follow all of them, if you don't know what they are, you might as well be playing the game with [all four paws] tied behind your back."

Found in the Historical Files, from the Ancient Year 2000
Gail Evans, Play Like a Man; Win Like a Woman

KITTY'S **K**ILLER **M**EMO

True to his word, Wolfe scheduled all of the interviews for the following week. Bright and early Monday morning, he met Kat in the large marble lobby of the Feline Food's Corporate Headquarters and escorted her to a cozy conference room on the fifth floor.

"I've got four felines scheduled to come talk to you over the next four days," he said gruffly.

"Talk to _us_," she corrected. "And their bosses are also coming in?"

"Yes," he replied, "but I'll tell you right up front, they aren't happy about having their decisions challenged."

"Wolfe!" hissed Kat in frustration, "I have no authority to 'challenge' them." Calming herself, she gave Wolfe an appealing smile, "You know I'm counting on your support in this. The canines aren't going to want to talk to me. I'll need your help to get them to open up."

Seeing him relax, she continued. "Who have we got coming in this morning?"

Wolfe pulled a handful of folders out of his well-worn leather dogbag. "Here are their personnel files. The one on top is coming in first."

Kat opened the thin file.

"Kitty Lyons." she mused aloud. "Let's see. She started working for the Company even before completing college. Hmm. She not only went to Rutweilers University, she graduated in the top ten percent of her class." Kat continued to peruse the file. "Her position with the Company is an 'In-Store Controller.' What is that?"

"It's a fancy name for the store's bookkeeper," replied Wolfe.

Kat looked puzzled. "I thought Feline Foods manufactured cat food. What's this about a 'store'?"

"Feline Foods is a huge conglomerate, Kat. We manufacture and retail a number of products related to the catfood we sell. A major outlet for our products is the chain of CatCo stores across the nation. Many are franchised, but we own a number of them."

"I see," said Kat. She returned her attention to Kitty's file. "Look at this. She's now a CPA – a certified public accountant. But she's still working in the same job--a 'bookkeeper' as you called it -- more than two years later?" Kat looked at Wolfe. "I wonder why?"

"So did I. That's why I picked her to interview," Wolfe replied.

There was a knock on the conference room door. Kitty Lyons stood in the doorway looking young but quite composed. She was sporting the latest in feline fashion-wear—a St. John Bernard suit.

"Please, come in," said Kat encouragingly. "You must be Kitty Lyons. I'm Kathryn Woo – please call me Kat."

Wolfe introduced himself, and Kitty took a seat.

"Thank you for coming," said Kat.

"I was told to report here this morning, but I have no idea why," said Kitty, her voice betraying both concern and irritation.

"Let me explain why we've asked you here," said Kat. Putting on her corporate face, she tried out the rehearsed explanation. "Mr. Rottweiler, the CEO of Feline Foods, has some concerns as to whether cats are adequately represented in the upper levels of management. He and Mr. Fyrum have engaged my services to study and analyze the dynamics governing Company patterns of feline promotions." (Ordinarily, Kat had no patience with such jargon – words intended to obfuscate rather than enlighten. Nonetheless, she understood the legal minefield inherent in canine-feline employment and was taking great care to protect her client.)

"As part of this study, we'll be interviewing a diverse group of associates who work for the Company. You just happen to be the first." Kat smiled encouragingly.

"The one thing we really need from you – from everyone we interview – is absolute candor. In exchange, let me assure you that everything you say today will be held in the strictest confidence."

Kat paused a moment and then asked, "Before we start, do you have any questions?"

"No," said Kitty. "But I'm very glad that Mr. Rottweiler is taking an interest in the problem."

"So you do see a problem?" said Kat, glad for the opening Kitty's statement had provided.

"Well, I was supposed to be promoted to corporate accounting more than a year ago, and it hasn't happened," said Kitty. "I'm still doing the same job I did when I started two years ago.

"Can I ask why a feline with your qualifications took a job as an 'in-store controller,'" Kat asked gently.

"Because Mr. Pointer told me it was only temporary. He promised that as soon as I passed the CPA exam, I'd be moved into the Accounting Department at Corporate Headquarters."

"Mr. Pointer?" said Kat, looking at Wolfe for clarification. "Is he the store manager?"

"No, he isn't," Wolfe replied. "Minerva Mouser is the store manager. Pointer is Vice President of Corporate Accounting. He hires all of the accounting associates, regardless of where they work."

"I see," said Kat. Turning back to Kitty, she continued with her questions. "So you didn't have your CPA license when you started?"

"No," replied Kitty. "The Company gave me the opportunity to work here while I completed my fifth year courses. I took the CPA exam after I finished the course work."

"Exactly when did you get your license?" asked Kat.

"A year ago." said Kitty flatly. "And I've been waiting ever since to make the move to Corporate Headquarters."

"Have you talked to anyone about it?" asked Kat. "Do you know why the promotion hasn't come through?"

"I know what Ms. Mouser *told* me," said Kitty. "First, she said that there weren't any openings in corporate accounting. But when I showed her a notice advertising *several* vacancies, she changed her story. She said that Mr. Pointer felt I needed more "seasoning"—that I needed a more thorough under-standing of the Company's accounting systems. But that's dog poop . . . I mean that's not true. I understood the system completely within my first six months. It's simple first-year bookkeeping!"

When Kitty didn't continue, Kat prompted her, "Well, if they didn't give you a valid reason for not promoting you, what do you think is really going on?"

"I don't know for sure," said Kitty. "But I think Ms. Mouser was unhappy about the memo I sent to Mr. Pointer about Cheetah Chihuahua."

Wolfe perked up. "'Cheetah Chihuahua'? You've got to be kidding. What, exactly, is a 'Cheetah Chihuahua'?"

"More to the point," said Kat with an exasperated look at Wolfe, "what was the memo about?"

Kitty took a deep breath. "Cheetah Chihuahua is a salesdog in our store. He was hired about a year ago. At first, everyone loved him. He was making more sales than anyone else in the store. Then, I figured out why. When I was recording his sales slips, I found he was discounting a lot of our high-end boutique merchandise – you know, the *Feline Foods* Cook-n-Eat, the Gourmet Kitchen items, and our signature Delight-in-Dining furniture collection."

"What do you mean, 'discounting,'" asked Kat.

"For one thing, he was honoring sales prices long after the sales were over. Other times, it looked as though he just *made up* prices, because some of them were *below cost,*" explained Kitty.

"What did you do when you discovered these sales slips?" asked Kat.

"Well, first I asked Ms. Mouser whether the sales staff was ever allowed to cut prices on their own."

"What did she say?" Wolfe asked, keenly interested in Kitty's story.

"She said, sometimes. But when I showed her Cheetah's sales slips, she got as upset as I was and said that he had no right to cut prices that often or that deeply. So I figured she would take care of it."

"And did she?" asked Kat.

"No. Two weeks later, I saw that Cheetah had written another sale at less than *half* the regular price. This time, when I went to Ms. Mouser, she said that she was 'handling the problem' and that I should leave it alone."

"And did you?"

"Yes – at first. At least I tried to. The rest of the sales staff was furious. They were losing customers to Cheetah, and they kept complaining to me. I told them Ms. Mouser was handling it, but time kept passing and nothing happened. Cheetah kept undercutting his fellow salesdogs and salescats until half of them were ready to quit. I told them to talk to Ms. Mouser, but I don't know whether any of them did. I only know that nothing happened, and Cheetah continued to cheat. Then, one evening, I saw Cheetah walking out to his car with an unopened carton of our Premium Plus cat food. I knew he lived alone, so I asked him why he'd bought so much. He said he didn't 'buy' it – he was just taking a few cartons. He said that it was 'okay' – but that I shouldn't say anything to anybody."

"That sounds a lot like stealing," said Wolfe. "What did Mouser say about that?"

"I tried to speak to Ms. Mouser, but she was traveling and didn't return my calls. I thought about waiting for her to get back, but what if she still didn't do anything? I know she's my boss, but, I mean, what Cheetah was doing wasn't right. It was hurting the Company. Anyway, I finally decided that I should let Mr. Pointer know what was going on. I wrote him a memo --with a copy to Ms. Mouser. I tried to avoid making it seem like any of this was Ms. Mouser's fault. And I explained that the only reason *I* was writing was because Ms. Mouser was away on official travel. Frankly, I thought that by making Mr. Pointer aware of the problem, he'd give Ms. Mouser the support she needed to get rid of Chihuahua."

"She didn't appreciate your efforts?" said Kat.

"I don't know. I never heard anything back from either Ms. Mouser or Mr. Pointer. The sales staff told me that Chihuahua got called on the carpet one Saturday morning, when I wasn't here. And he seems to be selling merchandise at the marked price, now. But ever since then, Ms. Mouser has been very cold and formal whenever we talk. She's always polite, but I can't help feeling that she's mad about the memo – I'm just not sure why."

"Did you ever ask her about it?" asked Kat.

"No," sighed Kitty. "I was hoping it was all in my imagination."

Kat finished making notes on Kitty's last comment and then said, "Kitty, thank you very much for being so forthright with us. It's been a big help. Is there anything else you'd like to add before we wrap up?"

"Is this study you're doing going to make any difference to me? I mean, is it possible you could get Mr. Pointer to find a position for me at corporate headquarters?" Kitty asked.

"Let me answer the second part of your question first," said Kat. "The answer is, no, we won't be making recommendations with respect to individual employees. As to whether the study we're doing will make any difference to you – I certainly *hope* so. I anticipate that the results of our work will have a *significant* impact on *future* promotions. I know that's not exactly what you hoped to hear, but don't give up. You've got excellent credentials. The Company can't afford *not* to promote employees of your caliber."

"Everyone should understand how things work on paper and how things actually work when they get a new job or enter a new organization."

Found in the Historical files, from the Year 2006
--by Carly Fiorina, *Tough Choices*

A PRINCE OF A BOSS

Princeton Pointer arrived at the conference room precisely at 11:00 a.m. Kat and Wolfe introduced themselves and explained their purpose. After completing the pleasantries, Wolfe began. "Prince, what can –"

"Princeton, my dear fellow," said Princeton Pointer. "I have never been a 'Prince', as I'm sure my employees will tell you."

Was he making a joke? It was hard to tell, and Wolfe decided not to risk a laugh. "Okay, then, Princeton. What can you tell us about Kitty Lyons?"

"Who?" said Princeton, sniffing at an errant piece of lint on his otherwise perfectly combed coat.

Kat picked up the conversation. "Kitty Lyons – she's the in-store controller of the Small City CatCo store." When Princeton continued to look confused, Kat continued. "She went to Rutweiler University.... finished her coursework and got her CPA license while working here. . . ." Still no flicker of recognition. "She sent you a memo about Cheetah Chihuahua–"

"Oh, yes," interrupted Princeton. "I remember her. Now I remember her."

When that was all he said, Kat continued. "Mr. Pointer, Ms. Lyons says she was promised a promotion to corporate finance as soon as she was licensed as a CPA."

"Ah, yes," said Princeton Pointer. "She didn't get that promotion, did she. No, no, and it's a shame. A real shame." Princeton slowly shook his head from side to side as if contemplating an avoidable tragedy. He looked up suddenly. "She's very bright, you know. Very bright."

"Then could you tell us why she wasn't promoted?" prompted Kat.

"Well, what does it say in her file? Her file should tell you, shouldn't it?" said Princeton.

At this point, Wolfe realized Princeton was not about to open up under Kat's gentle handling.

"Yes, Princeton," he said. "Her file says its because she couldn't understand the bookkeeping system after two years on the job—which is pure crap! Don't sit there and tell us she's very bright and then expect us to believe that you didn't promote her because she was too stupid for the job!"

Princeton looked offended. "Well, you know, now, that is, you know that very bright people can lack common sense, that is...."

"Knock it off, Princeton" said Wolfe abruptly. "Look, you've got a free pass this time – it doesn't *matter* why you didn't promote her. The only thing that *does* matter – the only thing that matters to *Bernie* – is that you tell us the true reason she didn't get promoted." Wolfe paused to let his message sink in, then continued.

"Now, we know she wrote you a memo about some salesdog named Cheetah Chihuahua. Did that have something to do with your decision not to promote her?"

Princeton eyed Wolfe, measuring his options. He finally decided, on balance, to tell the truth. After all, his reasons for not promoting Kitty Lyons were perfectly valid.

"Yes, yes. Of course it was the memo!" said Princeton with an air of resignation.

"What did it say that you found so objectionable?" asked Kat, rejoining the conversation.

"It wasn't what the memo *said*. It was the fact she wrote it at all. It exhibited very poor judgment on her part. Very poor judgment, indeed," said Pointer.

Kat tried again. "Mr. Pointer, it would help us to better understand the situation if you could tell us what was said in memo."

"Oh, of course. I thought you had a copy in the file," replied Pointer.

"It may be in *some* file, but it's not in hers," Wolfe interjected.

Pointer looked at Wolfe with distaste. "Perhaps not. Perhaps not. But you *will* find it in Cheetah Chihuahua's personnel file. Along with the reprimand we were forced to administer to him."

Kat was about to ask yet again for the substance of the memo when Pointer abruptly resumed speaking.

"Ms. Lyons' memo put it in writing—put it in *writing*, mind you—directly to me, that Cheetah Chihuahua was giving customers discounted rates without authorization," said Pointer.

"And, she implied that he was stealing—which was untrue, by the way."

Kat looked at him. "And this memo is a problem because. . .?"

"Because, Ms. Woo, that's not the way to do things. Not the way at all. In the first place, her memo made it appear as if the store were being badly managed, which reflected poorly on Ms. Mouser—and, indirectly, on me. In the second place, Ms. Lyons should have pursued this issue through the store manager. There is almost never justification for reporting problems directly to your boss's supervisor. But even if there were an excuse for bringing the problem directly to me, she should have talked to me privately, so that I would have had some flexibility in handling the matter. With everything spelled out in writing—on the record—my hands were tied."

"So, you're saying that you didn't promote Kitty Lyons because she put her concerns in writing instead of conveying them verbally?" asked Kat.

Pointer looked angry. "Of course not!" he huffed. "I'm saying she was given a direct order not to get involved in the situation with Chihuahua; Mouser said she was handling it! Apparently, Lyons felt compelled to take matters into her own hands. What that says to me is that she didn't trust her boss.

"Frankly, Ms. Woo, I would be very uncomfortable advancing an employee who so clearly lacks an understanding of the corporate hierarchy—someone who doesn't believe her boss is entitled to her trust or her loyalty.

"And, with respect to Ms. Lyon's unfortunate decision to catalog the poor chap's sins in writing, she managed to escalate a simple matter into a major issue—a major issue. We had to react much more strongly than was necessary. Yes, I know young Mr. Cheetah crossed the line in some of his actions. But in this economy, his efforts to boost sales showed some initiative. I could have channeled that initiative into a more appropriate direction. As it is, his future in this Company has been severely compromised. Severely compromised!"

Suddenly a thought struck Pointer. "You know, of course, who Cheetah Chihuahua *is*, don't you? Or should I say, who his father is?"

Seeing their expressions, Princeton continued. "Obviously, you do not. Cheetah Chihuahua is the son of Mr. Taco Chihuahua—Chairman Emeritus of the Board of Directors of Feline Foods."

Kat and Wolfe sat in shocked silence. Then Kat felt her anger come in a rush. "For Heaven's sake, why didn't someone tell Ms. Lyons that this prize salesdog was the son of the Chairman Emeritus of the Board? Wouldn't that have been the reasonable course of action!? And the fair thing to do."

"Frankly, it was none of her business!" said Princeton doggedly. "Ms. Lyon's poor judgment was not caused by Mr. Chihuahua's lineage. His being the son of a Board Member merely aggravated the damaging effect of her actions.

"Had she tended to her own business and permitted her supervisor to deal with the matter in her own time—as she was instructed to do—Mr. Chihuahua's transgressions would have been handled judiciously and none of us would have been put in this embarrassing position."

With that, Princeton Pointer rose and left the conference room without looking back.

"There is no way you can leapfrog, bypass, overrule, ignore, challenge, disobey or criticize your boss and not get penalized in the game."

Found in the Historical Files, from the Ancient Year 1980
Betty Lehan Harragan, <u>Knowing the Score</u>

K at & Wolfe Talk about the Rules

After lunch, Kat and Wolfe reconvened in the small conference room to go over the morning's interviews.

"Well," said Kat. "What do you think?"

"I think Pointer's an asshole," said Wolfe bluntly.

Kat resisted the temptation to say, "Now, tell me what you *really* think," and satisfied herself with, "Meaning. . .?"

"I think the meaning's clear enough. Personally, I find him arrogant, pompous, and irritating." Wolfe paused. "But he does have a point about Kitty Lyons. That memo was out of line."

"I agree," said Kat, somewhat to Wolfe's surprise.

"You do?"

"Yes, I do. Kitty shouldn't have written or sent the memo to Princeton. He was right to object to those actions."

Wolfe considered the matter. "Of course, it doesn't make a lot of sense to leave a CPA—someone of Kitty's caliber—in a job that doesn't begin to make use of her talents. It's a waste."

"True," said Kat, deliberately giving Wolfe time to think this through.

Apparently, Wolfe was finished thinking it through. "I give up!" he said, looking at Kat in frustration. "You're the expert. So tell me who's right—Kitty or Pointer?"

"It's not a matter of 'right' or 'wrong.' Each of them did what they thought was right, from their own very different perspectives."

"What perspectives?"

"Their perspective on the Rules of the Game—the unwritten rules that govern the workplace. Kitty hasn't learned the 'Rules of the Game', and Princeton doesn't realize the rules he plays by are 'unwritten.'"

Wolfe gave Kat a hard stare. "Well, he's not alone—*I* don't know what you're talking about!"

"Well, for one thing, the fact that Kitty sent a memo directly to Princeton Pointer rather than Ms. Mouser shows that she doesn't understand the rules of hierarchy—she doesn't understand the cardinal rule of a dog-run company: *never go over your boss's head.*"

Wolfe looked at Kat incredulously. "EVERYONE knows that," he said. "That's not an 'unwritten' rule. That's just. . . just OBVIOUS. I mean, if she doesn't even understand the sanctity of the boss/employee relationship, maybe she *shouldn't* be promoted."

"Yes, I guess you're right. . . . It was really foolish of Kitty to think that loyalty to her *Company* was more important than loyalty to her *boss*. . . ." Kat let her words hang in the air.

Wolfe furrowed his scruffy brow in thought. "I guess it may look that way in this case," he acknowledged. "But that's not the point. You defer to your boss because she has more information than you do. The boss has information that gives her the ability to make much more informed decisions—information she doesn't share with the employee—like who Chihuahua's father is!"

"Hmmm," mused Kat. "So, it's okay for Chihuahua to cheat because his father is on the Board of Directors?"

"Of course not!" said Wolfe, annoyed and confused. "It's just that . . . that the situation had to be handled more delicately. It's complicated. The whole thing is very complicated."

"EXACTLY!" said Kat. "Kitty Lyons made a decision to act in what she thought were the best interests of the Company, under very complicated circumstances. Making decisions is part of leadership. Explaining how and why a decision is wrong is part of *supervising*. The *question* is, why didn't Princeton Pointer do his job as a supervisor and *tell* Kitty that he thought writing the memo was a bad decision?!?"

"How would I know," grumbled Wolfe. "Maybe it was just easier to say she wasn't ready for promotion."

"That's probably true," granted Kat, hoping to appease Wolfe. "But I think there was another reason. Do you recall the first thing Princeton said after acknowledging that the memo was the reason she didn't get promoted? He said, that it showed 'very poor judgment' on her part."

"That's right," agreed Wolfe, recalling the conversation. "I remember agreeing with him."

"But, do you think *every* mistake an employee makes shows poor judgment?" asked Kat.

Wolfe thought about this for a moment and then said, "No, I guess not. So how was this different?"

"It's because she broke one of the cardinal 'rules of the game.' These unwritten rules are so ingrained in dogs—so obvious to the canines—that if an employee violates one of them, dogs automatically chalk it up to poor judgment."

"Okay," said Wolfe. "But even if that's true, what difference does it make to a supervisor. If Pointer thought Kitty made a mistake, whether it was because of poor judgment or poor accounting skills. why didn't he explain to her what she did wrong, and give her a chance to improve her performance?

"Because, unlike workplace 'skills, most supervisors believe that 'good judgment' can't be taught or learned. You either have it or you don't. Moreover, having 'good judgment' is essential for a professional or executive employee. Therefore, once an employee has shown 'poor judgment,' their career is often as good as over. Thus, when Princeton evaluated Kitty's writing the memo as 'poor judgment,' he automatically presumed it was not worth the effort of explaining her mistake to her because her 'poor judgment' was a permanent flaw—something she couldn't correct."

"Maybe he's right," said Wolfe. "Frankly, I don't think you *can* teach someone good judgment. Do you?"

"Maybe. Maybe not. But the ISSUE here is that Kitty's actions were *not* the result of 'poor judgment.'"

"I'm confused," fumed Wolfe. "Kitty violated one of the cardinal rules of the workplace when she went over her boss' head. You just said that when an employee breaks a rule like that it shows poor judgment. Now you're telling me its *not* poor judgment when *Kitty* does it?"

"Think of it like this. Suppose you're interviewing someone. He was born and raised in this country, but his speech is peppered with grammatical mistakes. You'd probably consider his failure to use proper English to be poor judgment—you'd assume he should know better. But suppose you're talking with someone who just emigrated from a foreign country, and he makes the same mistakes. I doubt you'd consider his mistakes 'poor judgment' —you'd assume that he hasn't learned all the rules of grammar, and *that he will*. You recognize that for the foreigner English is *a second language* and is a lot harder to learn as an adult.

"For cats, learning the unwritten rules of the canine workplace is like learning a new language. We can do it, given the chance."

"So we're not supposed to care that our feline employees are liable to make major errors in judgment?" fussed Wolfe. "We're just supposed to go ahead and promote them and *hope* that they "learn" these "unwritten rules" . . .

Kat stared at Wolfe. "Is that really what you think I've said, Wolfe?" she asked evenly.

Wolfe hung his head in frustration. "Okay. I apologize. It's just that first canines are told we're guilty of discatination because we haven't been treating felines like canines, so we make every effort to be sure both species are treated exactly alike. And now you come in here and tell me that we're guilty of discatination because we're not recognizing the *differences*! . . I don't know *what* we're supposed to do anymore."

Kat smiled. "That's <u>exactly</u> why I'm in business, Wolfe. I educate employees about the existence of these different perspectives and how to recognize when such a difference may be causing miscommunications – preferably *before* the damage is done."

Wolfe's expression remained grim. "Uh huh. And I suppose once we recognize these "differences" it's the canines who have to change what we say and how we do things."

"No," Kat said simply. "If the workplace is run by canines, they make the rules and those rules are going to match the nature of the beast – no disrespect intended," she added, grinning. "Besides, its extremely difficult to teach old dogs new tricks . . .

"Cats, on the other hand, are quite quick to catch on to new ideas and new ways of doing things. I teach felines not only what the "unwritten" rules are, but how to comply with them – how to look, speak and act in ways that convey competence – and *confidence* – to their canine bosses and counterparts.

"My biggest problem with cats is that they often complain they shouldn't *have* to comply with these 'unwritten rules.' Certain cats become hung up on how things 'should' be and refuse to accept the way things actually *are*. Nevertheless, once they understand how their bosses make decisions and how to *communicate* their competence to their canine bosses, even those felines have the *power* to manage their careers more successfully. The choice is theirs."

Kat opened her big pawbag and shuffled through a reef of papers.

"Here," she said, handing Wolfe a thin document. "This is the Tip Sheet I use in conjunction with the training course I offer to professionals just embarking on their careers – felines like Kitty Lyons."

Wolfe ran his eyes down the list of tips. "So all your training courses are for cats?" asked Wolfe, with his face full of hope.

"Training courses, yes," Said Kat. "But there's an educational portion of my training program that helps the canines who are in supervisory or managerial positions."

"What's the difference between a 'training' program and an 'educational' program?" asked Wolfe. "Just what kind of an 'education' are we supposed to get?"

"It's the education you're getting right now, Wolfe."

"Huh?"

"Sitting in on these interviews with me and talking about what's going on. You're learning *why* the felines are not being promoted; why they are being perceived as less competent than their canine counterparts," Kat explained.

"Yeah, I guess that's true to some extent. Although I'm not sure what good it's doing . . . unless you are going to expect me and the other executives to just overlook these 'differences,' as you call them."

Kat stared at Wolfe, then took a very deep breath.

"The expectation, Wolfe, is that once supervisors understand why their feline employees may act or react in ways that are unacceptable in the workplace, they can better *supervise* such employees. The greatest disservice a canine supervisor does to an employee is to assume that the feline is hopeless and refuse to be honest when he's unhappy with any part of her performance.

"The education I offer canines matches the training I offer felines so that when canine supervisors talk to feline employees about performance expectations, they're both speaking the same language."

Wolfe looked thoughtful. "Okay. I'll buy that. But I guess what I don't quite understand is how you 'train' someone like Kitty to act any differently than she did. I mean, what would you tell her she should have done instead of sending that memo?"

"Many an inept female gamester blames conflict-of-values when the real culprit is ignorance of the game rules, in this case, flouting the authority principles. Whether you personally agree with the game rules is largely irrelevant; when you decide to live in a foreign country you are obliged to conform with unfamiliar customs if you don't want to be ostracized by the natives."

Found in the Historical files, from the Year 1980
Betty Lehan Harragan, Knowing the Score

*L*essons for Kitty

The first years of a new career can be fun. Everything is new. Expectations are limited, giving you plenty of opportunity to exceed them. At the bottom of the ladder, there are is more opportunity and less competition. Indeed, business organizations are *looking* for promising employees to promote.

To succeed at this level, the first requirement is to *excel at your work.* Clearly, Kitty followed this lesson; she did good work.

The *second* lesson, however, is the one that Kitty did not follow—and that most felines fail to learn until well into the later years of their careers, if at all. Right from the first day, she must learn the "unwritten rules" of her workplace. These are the rules that tell her how to manage her career through the minefield of boss/employee interaction (often called the "politics" of work).

Why & How

If Kitty had understood the dangers of going over her boss's head, what could she have done differently?

There is no doubt that Kitty was facing one of the most difficult challenges of the workplace: being at odds with her boss over an issue of ethics. Nonetheless, there are ways she could have handled the situation.

Recruit Support

The best alternative for Kitty would have been to pursue her own suggestion that the sales staff go talk with Mouser. It's always helpful to have a "group" complaint, rather than an individual complaint. In other words, 'there's safety in numbers.' This alternative is dependent upon being able to convince or organize the salestaff into acting. The next alternative depends only upon Kitty.

Make the Case

Rather than writing the memo during Mouser's absence, Kitty should have waited and spoken to Ms. Mouser directly. This is a conversation that would require careful thought, planning and practice. Below is an example of what she might have said, broken into three parts:

First Statement

"Ms. Mouser, thank you for talking with me. I wanted to give you an update on a growing problem with Cheetah Chihuahua and see if there's any way I can help."

By offering to *help* rather than just complaining, Kitty is less likely to cause Mouser to become immediately defensive.

Second Statement

"I've followed your instructions and haven't mentioned anything to anyone. However, the sales staff knows what's going on and they've been complaining to me. I told them that you're handling the problem, but it's gotten to the point where Cheetah's cheating is affecting the atmosphere of the whole store. You've always focused on the importance of maintaining a collegial environment, so I wasn't sure you were aware of how much damage Cheetah's behavior is doing."

In this statement, she is focusing on what is important to *Ms. Mouser.* Kitty:

(1) Heeded Mouser's directions to let her handle it;

(2) Supported Mouser with the sales staff (by telling them that she is handling the problem);

(3) Compliments Mouser's leadership (maintaining a positive atmosphere; and

(4) Advises Mouser that Cheetah's actions are jeopardizing that collegiality.

Third Statement

"There is one other thing I need your help on. One evening while you were gone, I ran into Cheetah in the parking lot. He was putting a case of our Premium Brand catfood in his car. He admitted he didn't pay for it but told me that it was 'okay.'

"I haven't said anything because you asked me not to, but it puts me in a difficult position. We all had to sign the Company's Ethical Behavior Agreement when we were hired, and it requires us to report any clear evidence of wrongdoing. I just want to do the right thing. Can you help me?"

This statement communicates a new concern about Cheetah Chihuahua—that he may be a thief—and gives Kitty a valid reason to be bringing the topic to Mouser, again.

It also puts the issue into a whole new context for Mouser. Although it focuses on *Kitty's* concern about violating the company's ethical standards, it is effective because it invokes a 'higher authority.' The Ethical Behavior Agreement comes from corporate headquarters and the *concept* of ethics is taken seriously in most businesses. In a hierarchical organization, Mouser would not want to be perceived as someone who ignored the written rules of ethics. As Princeton Pointer noted, when something is in writing, it has a much more lasting and powerful impact.

What Happens Next?

Beginning and ending her comment with a request for Ms. Mouser's "help" is a relatively powerful way to force Mouser to commit to some sort of action. In general, there are three possible outcomes: Mouser commits to solve the problem and does; Mouser commits to solve the problem and doesn't; Mouser explains the problem. Let's look at how each of these would affect Kitty.

Mouser solves the problem. This is the optimum result . . . and not to be expected.

Mouser commits to solve the problem, but doesn't follow through in a timely fashion. From a career perspective, Kitty is in an excellent position. She has done her ethical duty by reporting what she's seen to her supervisor—not once, but twice. To be 'safe,' she should probably draft a short memo (yes, memo!) or email to Mouser thanking her for listening and for committing to resolve the issues with Mr. Chihuahua. It need not be more specific. The reason this memo is appropriate whereas the memo to Princeton Pointer was not is the recipient and the purpose. The memo to Mouser is what is often called a 'confirming' memo (or a "Memo for the Record") and is sent after a meeting or phone conversation to confirm that both parties had the same understanding of the meeting's outcome.

Mouser "explains" the problem. This is the most problematic result. It is possible that Mouser has already tried to get Princeton Pointer to give her the authority to reign in Mr. Chihuahua and that Princeton has told her to maintain the status quo. In this case, Mouser is in a worse position than Kitty, and she may look to share her guilt. She may tell Kitty that Cheetah is the son of the Chairman Emeritus of Feline Foods and that nothing is going to change.

In either of the last two cases, Kitty must determine her own level of corporate conscience. She has clearly complied with the written Ethical Standards Agreement: she reported wrongdoing. The Agreement she signed did *not* require an employee to go any further. The only reason for her to take any further action would be if she felt that Chihuahua's actions were so egregious that she could not, in clear conscience, stay silent. That is a personal choice.

CAREER MANAGEMENT 101:
"The Early Years: Getting Started"

Career Tips – Learn the Rules

1. Really good work will get you noticed; managing your career will get you promoted

2. Your boss is the key to your career success

3. For *career* success, pick a great boss over a great job

4. All employees have the same job description: "Do what your 'boss' wants done."

5. Get to know your boss – if you don't play golf, at least "do lunch" whenever possible.

6. <u>Spend</u> <u>time</u> planning appropriate ways to compliment and support your boss

7. If you "must" go over or around your boss, be prepared to keep on going out the door

8. Everything you say in the workplace will be heard by your boss.

9. Canine bosses consider "trust" and "personal loyalty" as the cornerstone attributes of an effective employee; without these, no amount of talent will advance your career.

_____

Part 3:
Look the Part

"The history of our wardrobe often reflects the history of our careers. One very smart [feline] I know can never really get ahead. Overweight, she dresses like a hippie in shapeless clothes designed to hide her body. Her company carefully moved her out of positions of power and excluded her from meeting with outside executives."

Found in the Historical data files, from the Year 2000.
Gail Evans, <u>Play Like a Man; Win Like a Woman.</u>

O BEESA MINDS THE STORE

Tuesday morning, Kat and Wolfe regrouped in the fifth floor conference room a little before their 10:00 o'clock appointment.

"Who's coming in this morning?" Kat asked.

"Obeesa Puss," said Wolfe, pawing through the batch of people-eared personnel files and handing one to Kat.

"What does she do?" asked Kat, as she picked up the file and started to read.

"She's a 'heavyweight' in retail management," replied Wolfe. Kat missed the smirk that flitted across his shaggy face.

"Let's see. . ." said Kat, as she ran her claw down the first page in the file, "it says here she has a degree in business and marketing. She was hired a little over ten years ago as a manager trainee, and she . . .wait, this can't be right." Kat looked up at Wolfe and then back down at the page in her paws. "It says she's been the *Assistant* Manager of Big City CatCo since 2995 – that's eight years. That's unheard of! Isn't the assistant manager position just a training ground for store managers? A two-or three-year stint?"

"Generally," said Wolfe, "which is –"

"Well, is she any good at what she does?" said Kat, unintentionally cutting Wolfe off as she grew increasingly interested in Obeesa' story.

"According to her reviews, she is," said Wolfe. "There are no complaints in her file, and she's had all K-1 ratings. This is why I picked her."

For the next 20 minutes, Kat read through Obeesa's file, concentrating on the annual evaluations. The file gave no clue as to why she'd been passed over.

At quarter past 10, Kat looked up and saw a pair of green eyes peering through the crack where the door stood slightly ajar. She waited a moment and then said to the doorway, "Obeesa?"

The eyes opened a bit wider, and a small, squeaky voice mewed, "Are you ready for me?"

"Yes. Please come in," replied Kat, who stood to greet the newcomer.

Obeesa gave the door a slight push, and it swung slowly inward, leaving Obeesa Puss framed in the open doorway of the conference room. Kat and Wolfe stared in amazement.

Obeesa Puss was a purebred Himalayan with an underactive thyroid. Her defensive response to the condition has always been to hide her weight behind outrageous attire. During her first few years with the Company, Obeesa shaved her midsection and wore the fur around her shoulders and haunches in long gelled spikes dyed blue and purple. When the punk cat look was no longer fashionable, Obeesa grew her fur out and had it permed into tight little curls, giving her the appearance of a short, fat poodle. After some of her friends hinted that she might want to strive for a more professional appearance, Obeesa had her fur straightened, but the effect was not exactly what she'd hoped for. Upon her return from the Beauti-Fur Salon, one of the salescats mentioned that "she looks like a piece of cotton candy," and for months thereafter everyone in the store called her 'Cotton Candy.' Her inch-long claws were painted red and clicked annoyingly as she walked.

This was the image that greeted Kat and Wolfe as Obeesa toddled into the room. Suddenly, Kat understood the double-entendre in Wolfe's reference to Obeesa as a 'heavyweight'—although it was impossible to tell if the approaching mass was composed primarily of cat or fur. Kat's anger flared; she wasn't sure whether she was angrier at Wolfe for his insensitivity or at Obeesa for her ignorance of corporate culture. Nonetheless, she reigned in her temper and stuck out her paw.

"Welcome, Obeesa. I'm Kat. And this is Wolfe"

"I'm Obeesa," said Obeesa barely touching Kat's paw with her own.

"Please have a seat, Obeesa" said Kat, suddenly wondering whether the chairs in the conference room were adequate for Obeesa's bulk. Kat hated herself for the thought, realizing instantly that Obeesa's weight was insignificant compared to some of the canines who used this room. It was just that she looked so. . . so. . . so round. . . or something.

Kat forced her attention back to the matter at hand. She quickly ran through the boilerplate introduction and asked a question to get Obeesa talking: "Tell me, how long have you worked for the company?"

"Oh, um, about 10 years," she said.

That didn't go far. Kat tried again. "Why don't you tell us a little about your career thus far, Obeesa?"

"There's not much to tell," said Obeesa, looking first toward the walls and then staring straight up at the ceiling. It was all Kat could do to stop herself from looking to see what was up there.

"Obeesa?" said Kat, trying to draw her attention from the ceiling.

"Oh. Sorry," said Obeesa, drawing her gaze down with difficulty and glancing at Kat out of the corner of her eyes. "I, uh, I've been at Big City CatCo the whole time. I'm the assistant manager. What else do you want me to tell you?"

Kat was frustrated. Obeesa seemed perfectly satisfied being an "assistant manager." If that's what she wanted to be, fine. But why would Wolfe have identified her as highly promotable if she wasn't interested? Apparently, the only way to find out was to be more direct.

"Obeesa, are you satisfied with your career here at Feline Foods?" Kat asked.

Obeesa looked down and swiped her paw across her small brown nose.

Kat imagined she could see the reluctance in her eyes – although she couldn't *actually* see more than a sliver of Obeesa's eyes under all the fur.

"It's okay, Obeesa. You won't get into trouble. Nothing you say will be attributed to you outside this room," Kat encouraged.

From somewhere under all that fur arose a backbone. "No, Ms. Kat, I'm not happy. I don't have a 'career' here. I've been an assistant manager for eight years. That's more than twice as long as anyone else has held that position. I do a better job than any of the assistant managers who were promoted last year... or the years before."

For the first time, Obeesa looked directly at Kat and there was a hint of fire in her eyes. "And you know what? I do a better job than most store *managers* in this Company. I'm here before 7 a.m. every morning and until 9 p.m. most nights. I've worked every holiday sale since I started, and Mr. Russell has put me in charge of merchandise, display, staff schedules and deliveries."

"Mr. Russell?" asked Kat.

"Jack Russell is the Store Manager," said Obeesa.

"What the heck is he doing while you're running the store?" asked Wolfe.

"Oh, he has a lot of meetings to go to at Corporate Headquarters," said Obeesa with what sounded to Kat like a trace of contempt.

"Meetings?" Kat asked, curious about what sounded like an aversion to meetings.

"Sometimes they're for training. But most of the time the meetings don't seem to have any real purpose. I went to one of the Senior Manager's meetings once. All they talked about were goals for the next five or ten years—and how the stock was doing. Stuff like that. I didn't learn anything that helped improve the store's sales volume. That's what *my* job is. And, frankly, I do it really well. Just ask me about the increases in our sales volume. Our store was # 1 in the country last year."

Kat marveled at the change that came over Obeesa when she talked about her work. She was a totally different cat –

strong and sure of herself. Kat dreaded asking the next question, but it had to be done.

"It's clear you're good at your job, Obeesa. So, I wonder if you have any thoughts as to why you haven't been given your own store?" Kat asked.

The energy that filled Obeesa when she talked about her *job* evaporated when the focus of the conversation turned to her *career*.

"I don't know," she answered, but the blush that colored the tips of Obeesa's fur a bright red said otherwise.

"Have you ever asked your boss about it?"

"Last year," she mumbled.

"What did he say?" prompted Kat.

"Well, he said he'd consider me. That my work was very good. But he didn't think I was ready for my own store."

"You didn't agree," Kat asked.

"No. But it doesn't matter. Karl Rover is next in line for his own store."

Wolfe spoke up for the first time. "Karl Rover? He just started with the Company a little over two years ago." Wolfe looked at Kat, who picked up on his thoughts.

"Obeesa," said Kat, "do you think Karl will be promoted first because he's a better manager than you are?"

"It's because he's a canine," Obeesa said without thinking, then began to turn three shades of red.

"Do you really think that's the reason, Obeesa?" Kat asked gently.

Obeesa looked down at her paws. "Not just that exactly. "It's more because Karl works out with Mr. Huntington at the Big City Catco gym and dog run."

"You can use the gym, too," said Wolfe naively. "They even opened up the dog run to both species just last year."

Obeesa looked up a Kat, in sheer misery. Tears seeped out of the bright green eyes and soaked Obeesa's beautiful cotton candy coat.

"I just can't do any of those things, Ms. Kat. I'm too . . . too busy. . . .and I just wouldn't feel right, you know?" Obeesa hung her head and let the tears flow.

Wolfe pictured Obeesa in a set of tights, trying to heft a set of barbells, or jogging around the dog run and suddenly realized that it had nothing to do with time or access. She was ashamed of her appearance.

> "Her fears, first reflected in her dress, have become a self-fulfilling prophecy."
>
> *Found in the Historical Files, from the Ancient Year 2000.*
> *Gail Evans, Play Like a Man; Win Like a Woman*

8

ASHFORD'S AVERSION TO COTTON CANDY

"So, tell me about Jack Russell," said Kat. It had taken Obeesa some time to calm down enough to leave the conference room. Now there were only a few minutes before their next interview, and Kat needed a quick run-down on Obeesa's supervisor.

"I can tell you about Jack Russell if you like," replied Wolfe impishly, "but that's not who's coming in."

"Why not? Isn't he Obeesa's boss?" asked Kat. "He's the only supervisor she mentioned."

"That may be part of the problem," Wolfe said. "Jack Russell is her boss, but it's *his* boss, the Senior Vice President of Retail Operations, who makes all of the decisions with respect to promotions. His name is Ashford Huntington."

At that moment, the door to the conference room opened, and Ashford J. Huntington III walked in. The moment he entered the conference room, Kat understood why Obeesa Puss had remained an Assistant Manager for so many years. Ashford, a prize-winning afghan, was the epitome of his breed – elegant, sophisticated, dignified, and aloof. His strikingly beautiful long silky coat was perfectly groomed, and he moved with the grace and agility of all such competitive hunters.

Kat noticed something else. The moment Ashford Huntington entered the room, Wolfe began reacting. He stretched his large frame to its fullest; his ears stood perfectly straight; and he quietly shoved his crutch under the table. Kat wondered whether there was history between the two or merely a natural canine competitiveness.

Ashford greeted Wolfe pleasantly. "Wolfe—good to see you back on your feet. How's the knee?"

"Doing great, Ashford," replied Wolfe, not the least inclined to discuss his infirmity. "Have a seat. I'll try to get you out of here as fast as possible." Wolfe knew by the look on Kat's face that he had blundered. To his credit, he made an effort to undo the damage. "This project is Bernie's top priority right now, so I know you'll give us your full cooperation."

"I'm not sure I understand what it is you want from me. I've promoted a number of felines to the position of store manager. Frankly, they do just as well as the canines," said Ashford sounding genuine. "The only thing I look at is the bottom line – I don't care who's running the store as long as it shows continuous increases in volume and profit."

Kat walked forward to introduce herself.

"Mr. Huntington, I'm Kathryn Woo," she extended her paw, which was immediately swallowed up in the long fur of Ashford's forepaw. "Please call me Kat."

"Ms. Woo – Kat – I'm delighted to meet you – I didn't see you when I came in; please forgive my boorish behavior." He smiled, and again Kat felt genuine warmth in his greeting. "Wolfe has a tendency to bring out the worst in me. – And please call me Ashford."

"All right – Ashford. Please understand that we aren't here to find fault with you or any of the Company executives. All we're doing right now is collecting information to see if we can determine why the Company doesn't have more felines in upper management."

"Well, store managers certainly aren't considered 'upper management,' noted Ashford.

"That's very true," responded Kat. "But to get the answers we're looking for, we need to understand how promotion decisions are made throughout the employee's career."

"That makes sense," said Ashford. "How can I help?"

Kat smiled. She liked this dog. "What we need from you is some information about one of your employees who's been an assistant manager for eight years – Obeesa Puss. Do you know her?"

"Of course I know her," Ashford answered pleasantly. "I know all of my managers and assistants – and most of the sales staff in the stores. I don't know Ms. Puss as well as many of the others, since she seldom comes to corporate, but I do know her."

"Then what's the story – why has she been an 'assistant' manager for more than eight years?" said Wolfe, rather aggressively. "Shouldn't she be a store manager by now?"

Unphased, Ashford turned so that he could address both Kat and Wolfe. "Ms. Puss is a competent assistant manager. But right now, I have no plans to promote her."

"Could you tell us why?" said Kat, encouragingly.

"Well, there are two reasons," said Ashford. "First, I am strongly guided by the store manager's assessment in making promotion decisions. Obeesa's store manager – Jack Russell – is firmly convinced that she lacks the temperament – the confidence – to manage a store on her own. He rates her administrative skills very highly, but as you both know, management requires much more than being able to keep the store stocked with the right merchandise."

"What's the second reason?" asked Wolfe.

"I understand you met with Ms. Puss earlier this morning?" said Ashford.

"Yes, we did," replied Kat.

"Then you will understand when I say that I have a serious concern about her appearance," said Ashford, without sounding judgmental. "Store managers are our Company's primary representatives to the public. I'm not at all convinced that Obeesa Puss is the image we want the public to associate with Feline Foods."

"Don't you think that's a little unfair, Ashford," said Wolfe. "She can't help being . . . being overweight. Himalayas are big to begin with. Do you think it's right to penalize her for her looks?

"And isn't there a *legal* issue involved?" continued Wolfe with added zeal. "I mean, if her size is because of her breed, isn't that an illegal form of discatination. . .?"

"I said nothing about her size or her weight, Wolfe," said Ashford, clearly and forcefully. "What I said is that I question her *appearance*. Over the eight years she's worked in Big City CatCo, she has gone from looking like a member of 'Hell's Angels' to looking like a bag of popcorn to her current appearance, which has won her the nickname 'Cotton Candy'! I have no problem with her *weight*. We are all endowed with different body types. and we must deal with those differences. What I do have a problem with is how she chooses to *attire* and *present* that body."

"So what are you suggesting she *do* about it, Ashford?" retorted Wolfe sarcastically, "wear a girdle?"

Still refusing to rise to the bait, Ashford answered with surprising equanimity.

"Do you recall Max Moocher, the bulldog who was Vice President of Sales and Marketing until just recently? He was at least 50 pounds overweight – far heavier than Ms. Puss, pound for pound. The difference is that Max had his fur custom tailored to minimize his bulk and to make the most of his looks – and he wore attire that enhanced his looks. Frankly, I have no idea whether Ms. Puss is overweight – but the manner in which she grooms her fur accentuates her size in a most unflattering manner! And her decision to do that, Mr. Wolfhound, is a matter of judgment!"

Kat jumped in before Wolfe could respond. "Ashford, I have just two more questions. First, did you – or did Jack Russell – ever tell Ms. Puss that she should try to look more professional in her appearance?"

"Actually, Kat, I don't believe either one of us had that conversation with her." To his credit, Ashford looked mildly embarrassed. "But I do know that at some point her co-workers made that suggestion. I think that was when her fur was in a mass of tight little curls. . . Unfortunately, their comments apparently led to this current look. So I'm not sure it would have helped if either Jack or I had said something."

"Possibly not," said Kat. "Of course, the suggestion of a *supervisor* certainly carries more weight with an employee."

She realized the unintended pun immediately, but it was too late to undo the damage. Best to simply move along, she thought quickly.

"There's one other thing I need to know."

"Go right ahead, Kat" said Ashford, smiling in spite of himself.

"Please don't take this the wrong way," said Kat, embarrassed to realize that she was hedging her questions in order not to offend Ashford. "You said you rely heavily on the evaluations that the store managers give their assistants," she continued.

"That's right," agreed Ashford.

"Do you also take into account the fact that the managers making those evaluations might have conflicting motivations?"

"What are you suggesting?" asked Ashford.

"I'm suggesting that the better an assistant manager is, the more the store manager may want to *keep* him – or her. Isn't it possible that this self-interest might influence a manager's evaluation?"

"It's possible, Kat," acknowledged Ashford. "In fact, it's happened in the past. That's why I try to get to know the assistant managers for myself – as a check on what my managers are telling me. Unfortunately, Obeesa has never taken advantage of the opportunities we provide for all the managers to network with me and the other corporate executives, so I've only seen her when I visit the store. Even then, she is often unwilling to stop working long enough to say, hello. And while I applaud her diligence, I would again have to question her judgment."

Ashford paused for a moment, and then continued. "She just doesn't seem to have any sense about what's good for her own career."

"Yes," said Kat. "I think that's painfully clear."

> "If you don't look the part, you won't be recognized as a competent professional no matter how smart or educated you are."
>
> *Found in the Historical files, from the Ancient Year 2000.*
> *Lois Frankel, Nice Girls Don't Get the Corner Office*

KAT & WOLFE TALK ABOUT 'PROFESSIONAL PRESENCE'

"That canine is a snob," said Wolfe as Ashford disappeared into the elevator.

Kat look surprised. "What makes you say that, Wolfe?"

"Just because he looks like a TV model, he belittles any species that doesn't."

Kat allowed her gaze to wander over the scruffy coat shared by all wolfhounds. No, life wasn't fair, she thought. On the other hand, looking "scruffy" certainly hadn't hindered Wolfe's career. But she could understand his jealousy and decided just to ignore it.

"So, would you promote Obeesa if it were your decision—and your responsibility?" asked Kat, refocusing the conversation.

Wolfe thought about it. "Well, she definitely needs some improvement in her appearance, but I liked the determination she showed when she talked about her job. I think she'd be a good store manager."

"I agree with you," said Kat, smiling.

"You do" said Wolfe. "So, I'm right, and Afghan's wrong?"

"Not exactly," replied Kat. "You have an advantage over Afghan. You actually communicated with Obeesa. I doubt he's ever heard her say much of anything, let alone brag about her abilities like she did with us."

"I wouldn't call that 'bragging'" said Wolfe.

Kat held up a paw. "Don't misunderstand! I'm not insulting Obeesa—I'm complimenting her. For cats, 'bragging' is a good thing. Part of my training involves teaching felines how to 'toot their own horn,' so to speak."

Once again, Kat refocused the discussion. "You said something about Obeesa's appearance. What's your thinking about that?"

"Well, I guess I have to agree with Afghan on that; he put it right on the money. She needs to use better judgment in looking more professional." Wolfe looked thoughtful. Then he asked Kat, "Does your training deal with this kind of thing? I mean, telling someone—anyone—that they don't dress right isn't easy."

Kat smiled; Wolfe actually asked about her training. This was progress.

"You may not be aware of this, Wolfe, but there was a famous book from the Ancient Years called *Dress for Success*— one for women people and one for men people. The book was very limited in its advice, but it initiated the concept that what employees wear at work has a significant impact on how they are perceived and how successful they'll be.

"And, yes, I do talk about this in one of my training courses –choice of attire plus a number of other things. An employee's appearance is a great deal more than just what he or she wears. Granted, Obeesa's unique designer fur tends to overwhelm her presence, but do you recall anything else about her that made an impression on you this morning?"

It didn't take Wolfe long to respond. "You mean the fact that she stood out in the hall for who knows how long before knocking? Or the way she stared at the ceiling for most of the interview? Or that she squeaked like a sick mouse when she first got here?"

"Exactly," said Kat. "Everything about Obeesa gave the impression that she lacks the confidence to tie her shoes, much less manage a store. Most of these behaviors are the type of things we all do without thinking. During training, employees like Obeesa learn two things: (1) how to use external accoutrements (dress, jewelry, briefcase, etc.) to create a professional appearance, and (2) how to use their *bodies* (how to stand, sit, walk, gesture, smile, etc.) to create a professional appearance."

Wolfe looked skeptical. "I still don't know how you turn a feline as terrified and timid as Obeesa into a confident cat. But I agree with your premise that unless somebody *can* fix employees like Obeesa, they aren't going to have a lot of success.

"Actually, Wolfe, the training program will be successful whether or not Obeesa is "fixed," as you so delicately put it."

Before Wolfe could argue, Kat continued.

"Let me explain. Right now, most felines just don't understand what they're doing wrong. Kitty didn't understand the hierarchy rules we talked about yesterday. Obeesa obviously doesn't understand the rules of professional appearance, nor does she understand how to manage her career. What the cats *do* understand is that they do really great "work" and don't get promoted. They see canines who work fewer hours and produce fewer sales getting promoted to jobs for which the felines feel they are clearly more qualified.

"Not understanding *why* tends to make the felines angry and unhappy. And as Bernie is learning, this anger and unhappiness will ultimately manifest itself in decreased productivity (at best) and discatination lawsuits (at worst)."

"All right, all right. You've said this before. So what's your point?" Wolfe was not a patient dog.

"My point, Wolfe, is that by enlightening felines about what's expected of them in the workplace *beyond* doing a good job, teaching them "unwritten rules," and training them how to manage their careers, felines are *empowered* to make choices. Some of them will jump right into the game, master the unwritten rules, and become natural candidates for promotion. Some of the felines will decide they have no interest in playing by your rules and will opt out of the corporate culture, even start their own businesses. And some will decide they don't want to change the way they dress or act, but will decide that they are happy with the job they have and don't need to be in constant competition for promotion.

"The one thing that the training program will do for all of your feline employees is to give felines the knowledge and ability to understand how and why most promotion decisions are made and the tools to compete with their canine counterparts. The decision as to whether or not they want to compete is then theirs."

"So you're saying that after they take your course, all of the felines will be happy and content?" said Wolfe.

Kat smiled. "If you want all "happy cats," try catnip. There will *always* be employees – of both species—who are unhappy with work. Poor supervision is the most common reason, by the way. With respect to the effect of my training, there will be some cats who don't want to hear what I have to say. They won't accept that they should have to play by your rules. They will continue to insist that there should be "objective" criteria for promotion (as if there were such a thing). They will refuse to change anything about themselves and will continue to be angry when they're passed over."

"Sounds like these are the dumber members of your species," offered Wolfe.

"Actually, Wolfe, these are the felines that will eventually change the workplace. Someday you'll have to play by *their* rules," said Kat. "These are the cats who are responsible for initiating things like the Feline Integration Project. Without them to push for change, there would never have been any. But they continue to want change now, and at this point, their confrontational approach can be quite damaging. I just don't think that's necessary in today's world.

"Today, most companies, like Feline Foods, have seen the results of feline integration; they've seen the statistics showing companies with a significant percentage of felines in upper management have measurably higher performance data and are more profitable. They want more cats. They just need help getting it done.

"What most canines and felines don't understand is that the very thing that makes "diversity" valuable is what makes it so hard. Bringing together species with different perspectives and life experiences provides great value in coming up with business solutions and marketing products. However, it also creates a real challenge for these diverse employees to *communicate* successfully with one another when they may not only speak a different language but often hold very different views about the ways in which employees interact in the workplace."

Wolfe was smiling.

"You really get quite passionate about this topic, don't you," he said.

Kat was embarrassed. "I'm sorry, Wolfe. I didn't mean to get so carried away. Did I sound like a I was preaching?"

"Maybe," said Wolfe with a big grin. "But if so, you're making me an acolyte."

Kat couldn't believe it! Wolfe was becoming a convert. An amazing thing, passion.

"Okay," Wolfe continued. "Can you show me some training lessons for Obeesa, like you did for Kitty?"

"Competence and smarts won't do you much good if no one knows you have them. Substance without style and presence is largely lost on those you hope to impress. To make it to the top and stay there, you must not only <u>be</u> capable, effective, and intelligent, you must <u>look</u> as if you are."

Found in the Historical Files, from the Ancient Year 1992
D.A Benton, <u>Lions Don't Need to Roar</u>

*L*essons for Obeesa

Why and How

Obeesa needs to understand (1) the reason for looking professional and (2) the reason for being *visible* at corporate meetings. At the same time, it is important to teach her *how* to look professional and *how* to showcase herself at corporate meetings. Learning *why* these things are important only breeds frustration if she doesn't know *how*. Learning *how* to do these things has no value if she sees no reason to change.

I.   LOOK PROFESSIONAL

A good starting place for any learning experience is to read up on the topic. One of the best books on the subject of "professional presence" is *Lions Don't Need to Roar: Using the Leadership Power of Professional Presence to Stand Out, Fit in and Move Ahead*, by Debra Benton. Her practical work explains the value of 'professional presence' and provides a treasure chest of detailed instructions on how to obtain it.

The essence of 'professional presence' is controlling your appearance and your physical movements to create the perception that you are calm and in control. Those who are calm and in control are perceived as being confident. There are many aspects of professional presence.

The Uniform

- *Clothes.* The basic rule is to dress for the job you want rather than the job you have. A second fundamental rule of dress is to buy clothes not for how *they* look, but for how they make *you* look. Finally, the 'appropriateness' of clothes is based on the practice and style of your particular workplace.
- *Jewelry.* The basic rule for wearing jewelry in the workplace is, 'less is more.' A second fundamental rule is to make fewer purchases but buy 'good' jewelry rather than costume jewelry for the workplace.

Obeesa needs to observe what well-respected feline store managers are wearing and pattern her own wardrobe after theirs. If there's a particular manager Obeesa trusts, asking for her help shopping is a good way to get started.

Professional Presence

- *Posture.* The basic rule of posture is 'Your mother was right'—good posture is essential in creating a professional presence. It is the first ingredient in looking relaxed and in control.

> "Good posture makes you look confident, successful, appropriately energetic—and taller."
>
> *Lions Don't Need To Roar*, p.54

- *The Tilt of Your Head.* The basic rule is: DON'T! Keep your head level and relatively still. As trivial as this may seem, remember that others form their impression of you within the first moments of meeting you.

> ➤ "A bowed head conveys insecurity, shyness, and defeat."
>
> ➤ "A cocked head conveys confusion and simple-mindedness."
>
> *Lions Don't Need To Roar*, p.31

- *The Eyes Have It.* Look directly at the person you're meeting or talking with. This tells them that they have your complete attention. Maintain eye contact an "appropriate" length of time—you don't want to make someone uncomfortable by staring at them unblinking. Then smile—your eyes will twinkle and your personality will shine.

- *How to Stand*

1. Maintain a relaxed, energetic posture with eyes and head level.

2. Assume a neutral or "ready" position with your arms loose at your sides so they are free to gesture. Keep your hands out of your pockets and do not cover your crotch or fold your arms across your chest.

3. Stand close enough to the other person to be personal, but not so close as to be intrusive.

4. Stand upright rather than leaning against a door, wall, lectern, or furniture. The former position makes you look solid and sure of yourself. You'll look uncertain and easy to sway if you lean.

5. Don't touch yourself or pick real or imaginary lint off your sleeves; smooth your clothing; tug at your waistband; straighten your tie; fuss with your hair; or rub your hands (like Lady Macbeth attempting to scrub off the "damned spot).

Lions Don't Need To Roar, p. 54

Practice! Practice! Practice!

Reading "how to stand" is fine, but you won't change your stance *just* by reading how to. The best, indeed, the only way to become comfortable with any new physical skill is to do it over and over until the actions come naturally.

One of the best ways to practice these skills is in front of a mirror. Stand in front of a large (preferably full length) mirror in the privacy of your home and pretend you're conversing with a business acquaintance. Observe your posture; see how you hold your head; watch how you move your eyes. It may be uncomfortable, at first, because if you're like most felines, you aren't used to focusing so much attention on yourself (except, perhaps, when you are applying make-up).

An even better practice tool is the video camera. Use a trusted friend—or a tripod—and capture yourself walking and talking. Then sit down, watch the results, and do an honest evaluation of what you see.

Finally, as you begin to incorporate these skills into your repertoire at work, it helps to keep track of your progress. Create a chart to log your successes. Make a note of every time you successfully incorporate one of the skills you want to acquire into your workday.

There's no set way to track things. For example, under "practice good posture," a 'success' might be each time you remember to straighten that back and lift those shoulders when you're walking out of your office and into areas where you will see and be seen by others.

Other Suggestions

For someone such as Obeesa who currently projects very little confidence in the way she presents herself, it might be worth hiring an Executive Coach. She will need a lot of encouragement to make these changes. We know that she has the ability to project a confident image when she's talking about her *work;* what she has to learn is to project the same confidence when she's talking about *herself.*

II.   BE VISIBLE

In larger organizations, such as Feline Foods, you often have more than one "boss." For example, the store manager is Obeesa's direct boss, but *his* boss, Ashford Huntington, makes all of the promotion decisions. While Obeesa must remain loyal to Jack Russell, she must become known to those further up the chain of command. Managing your career requires you to be *visible* to the senior executives. Corporate meetings are one of the best venues to see and be seen.

Why Be Visible?

Regardless of what Canine-Feline Resources says about a company's "fair and objective" evaluation process, the canine [human] factor will trump every time. Obeesa needs to understand that as a mid-level manager, her career success will now be based on perceptions and relationships; doing a good job is no longer enough.

> "Let's be real: Every workplace is political, and the higher up the organizational chart you go, the more political the workplace gets. That's because there's more at stake. The higher up you go, the more things get accomplished by virtue of relationships and positioning."
>
> Mary Foley, <u>*Bodacious! Career,*</u> *p.134*

One of the first recommendations for Obeesa is to read <u>Tough Choices</u>, by Carly Fiorina, a former CEO of Hewlitt-

Packard, a huge computer company in the 21st century. Ms. Fiorina's real-life stories of how the workplace actually functions are insightful—particularly the company's evaluation process.

Once a year, mid-level managers met together to rate and rank their employees. To prepare for her first meeting as a mid-level manager, Carly asked two of her more experienced peers to describe the process. Here is what happened.

Feline-Speak

> "I went to Marie . . .who'd always been so helpful to me in my previous job. She described a very rational, thorough process in which the supervisors presented their employees and proposed ratings and rankings. When they had completed their presentations, there was a general discussion and then everyone came to an eventual agreement on the distribution of the ratings and how each employee was ranked in the total universe. Sometimes they also talked about an employee's potential to move up in the organization."
>
> *Tough Choices,* p.41

Canine-Speak

> "Then I talked to Ron Ketner.... 'Listen, Carly, I don't know what Marie told you, but here's the bottom line. Rating and ranking is just a big horse-trading session. Every boss wants to be sure to have as many of their people at the top as possible; otherwise they don't look good to their own boss when it's their turn to get rated and ranked. So we're all competing against each other in that room, and you have to do your friends some favors if you want them to do you some. . . this is politics pure and simple.'"
>
> *Tough Choices,* p.41

What Carly Learned at the Evaluation Meeting

"I learned a lot about how things actually worked. First, just because someone was a second-level didn't mean they were any smarter than a first-level. ...As someone who had never been in a big corporation before, I'd just assumed that level and title must have some correlation to character and capability. ...I found out that day that I was wrong.

. . .

"Managers seemed more enthusiastic about subordinates with whom they were comfortable...those subordinates who were a lot like the bosses in their habits and interests, or subordinates who fit the bosses' image of what success looked like; these employees did much better in the rating and ranking than those who were different, or challenging, or less well known. If a boss was uncomfortable with a subordinate, it showed up in how he talked about her or him.

"When you're thinking about whether you're comfortable with someone, you focus on their personality and characteristics. *So looking and acting the part could also win out.*"

<u>Tough Choices</u>, p. 42-43.

Being "visible" is a key element of "managing" your career.

How to Be Visible

Corporate gatherings – particularly corporate meetings – provide a unique opportunity to be "visible" to the corporate hierarchy. For someone such as Obeesa who is not a natural extrovert, the thought of being "visible" in such an environment may be quite intimidating. Here are some ways to minimize that angst.

1.   *Meet and Greet.* The best way to enter the world of corporate gatherings is with a mentor who can introduce you to others. If the company has a mentoring program, this should be one of their first tasks. The mentor does not have to be in a formal relationship, however. If Obeesa has a friend or a trusted co-worker who attends these meetings, he or she can serve this role and provide initial introductions.

2.   *Speak Up.* Corporate meetings provide a wonderful showcase for employees to be heard as well as seen by the higher-ups. Even with a very large group, there are opportunities to answer questions and offer ideas or opinions.

Obeesa is most comfortable and confident talking about the success of her store. There are no doubt a number of useful success stories she could contribute. To generate enough confidence to speak up in such a setting, Obeesa needs to:

- Prepare
- Think
- Plan
- Rehearse
- Implement

Prepare. Find out what the format of the meeting will be. Who will be speaking? What is the theme of the meeting? What specific topics will be covered? Do the speakers take questions? Is there any other type of audience participation? If so, do you speak from your seat? Do you go to a microphone in the aisle? What kinds of questions have gotten good (or bad) responses in previous meetings?

Think. Process all the information you've learned about the meeting and think about how your personal knowledge and experience fits into the theme. Think about what you know that would clearly benefit others in your company. (Think about all the times you've said, "I can't *believe* they don't do "X" in the other stores!") Think about a way to work your comment into a "question."

Plan. Decide on one or two particular messages, ideas or opinions relevant to the theme of the meeting that you'd like to express, given the opportunity. Work them into a 'question' and write out a concise summary of your points; write like you would speak.

Rehearse. Read your summaries aloud to yourself or a trusted family member or friend. Continue to practice until you know the material by heart *and* you sound completely natural.

Implement. During the meeting, listen carefully to what's being said, looking for the right opportunity to contribute. It's possible that the right opportunity won't arise at that meeting, but opportunity only knocks on the door of those who are prepared to take advantage of it.

If you think you're still going to have trouble forcing yourself to stand up and speak, use your mentor/friend. Before the formal part of the meeting, tell them what you would like to contribute and ask for their help. When the right opportunity comes along, your mentor can stand and tell the group that he/she was "talking to Obeesa Puss and she had a great idea that I'd like her to share." Then, it's all up to you!

3.   *Follow Up.* After the meeting, take the time to review whom you've met. Make notes about conversations that you want to remember. List (and do) anything you promised others. Send a short hand-written note (or email, depending upon your

company's culture) to anyone with whom you felt you'd made a connection. It doesn't need to say anything more than: *"It was great to meet you yesterday. Let me know if I can ever be of help."*

4.   *Build Relationships.* Set a goal to create one new working relationship from each major corporate meeting. As you meet new [people], select someone with whom you feel a connection. It may be a peer who shares your same job—and your same issues. It may be someone at the next level who's been where you are and can share advice. It may be someone on their way up whom you can mentor. Cultivate professional relationships by 'doing lunch' or touring your store. Look for other professsional opportunities to attend together.

The most difficult challenge for most felines such as Obeesa who value and enjoy doing a great job at their 'work,' is taking the TIME to 'be visible' or to do any of the things which are critical to managing a career.

Managing your career *takes* time. Your career is *worth* taking time for.

CAREER MANAGEMENT 201:
"The Middle Years"

Career Tips – Look the Part

Create a Professional Presence

- Each job level has a "uniform;" wear the uniform that matches the job you want to be perceived as having.

- The right attire *gives* you more power than you actually have; the wrong attire *robs* you of the power you do have.

- Everything you wear sends a message.

- You should not jingle, jangle, dangle, or click when you walk.

- Don't groom yourself in public.

- Make-up is the backdrop of a beautiful picture; it should enhance what is seen but never be seen.

- Maintain eye contact, but don't engage in a staring contest.

- Sit with power, near power.

- Take up space; make your presence felt.

- Use your mirror for more than makeup; use it to practice walking, sitting, standing, and speaking.

- Smiles are valuable; use them wisely.

- Your walk should be grounded and stable; don't swing, sway, bounce, or weave.

Part 4:

Speak the Language

"Talking, like walking, is something we do without stopping to question how we are doing it. In a situation in which one person is judging another . . . the consequences of style differences can be dire indeed."

Found in the Historical Files, from Ancient Year 1994 by Deborah Tannen Talking from 9 to 5

HAVANA GETS KICKED OUT OF THE SANDBOX

Havana Brown hurried into the conference room, threw herself into a chair, and looked at the watch on her long brown forepaw.

"Sorry I'm late," she began, breathlessly. "The lawyer representing one of our former employees called me just as I was running out the door. It's an uncivil rights case. Sophie Sphynx —she's the employee who's suing us—says that she was fired because of her breed. (Who could *blame* her boss if she *did*. I mean, that's one *ugly* breed of cats!) Anyway, the case is getting ready to go to court and Freddy Thompson – that's the lawyer who called me – he wanted to put an offer on the table before I put any more work into the trial. Not that it was *much* of an offer – still way over our budget for these things. We try to keep payouts under $100,000 – even though we'd probably win at trial, the time and cost of going to court is generally just not worth it – but you all know that, I'm sure."

Havana, who had delivered this monolog in one breath, paused, and Kat took quick advantage of the break.

"Don't worry about the time, Havana. You're not *that* late, and we have all morning. Thank you for taking the time to come talk with us. I'm Kathryn Woo, by the way. Please call me Kat."

Havana reached her foreleg across the table to touch Kat's outstretched paw.

"It's nice to meet you, Kat. And it's so good to see Wolfe again. Wolfe and I worked on one of his special projects together, what—two, three years ago?" she asked, turning to Wolfe. "We made a great team, didn't we?" said Havana, with a wink.

"We kicked their tails!" said Wolfe, grinning widely.

Havana turned her attention back to Kat. "So, what's the deal with you two? I hear you're trying to get the canines to promote more cats. Any luck so far?"

"It's too early to tell," said Kat. Then, seizing the opening, she asked Havana, "What do you think are our chances?"

"Oh, somewhere between 'null' and 'void'," said Havana, drawing upon her legal lexicon to express her cynicism.

Wolfe looked at Havana. "You know, people told me you were unhappy with the Company, but I had a hard time believing them. When we worked together, you were the Company's biggest cheerleader. What happened to turn you into such a cynic?"

"I got kicked out of the Sandbox case, Wolfe," she said. "*That's* what happened. I had the rug pulled out from under me on the biggest case of my professional life! No warning – no discussion about *why* I was being replaced. Yes, you could call me cynical!"

Kat took control of the conversation at that point and asked Havana to back up and walk them slowly through everything that happened, starting with an explanation of the "Sandbox" case.

"Okay," she replied. "I've written out the facts of the case so many times, it'll sound like I'm reciting from memory—but here goes."

And so saying, she began.

"Three years ago, on December 31, 2999, the Minneapolis CatCo Store was in the midst of the Company-wide 30th Century Centennial Sale. Among the many customers who came through the store that day was a Munchkin kitten and her parents. They were being waited on by Buddy Bassett, who was enjoying his last day of work before retirement. Buddy moved slowly under the best of circumstances and had slowed to a virtual crawl in his waning years.

"After two hours of shopping, Munchkin's parents were testy and on edge, and Munchkin had wandered off, looking for a place to relieve herself. Low and behold, the kitten came upon a 15-foot high display of the store's newest litter facility, called the "Super Sandbox." Hundreds of these things were stacked criss-cross and crossways, in a free-for-all fashion designed and erected by the dyslexic stockdog the store hired for the holidays. Needless to say, Munchkin was thrilled with the discovery. She spotted a bright red one right in middle of the Super Sandbox Tower and—red being her favorite color—clawed her way up the stack, sat herself down, and began, well, *using* it. This unanticipated activity put an unexpected stress on the delicately balanced Tower, and it began to lean precariously to the left.

"Suddenly, Munchkin's parents looked up and spied their kitten just as she hopped tidily out of the Super Sandbox.

Munchkin's father stood watching in wide-eyed amazement as his wife, who, believing the tower was about to fall and crush her baby, sprang full out onto the wobbling tower, grabbed the kitten in her teeth, and leaped clear of the emerging disaster. The weight of a full-grown feline using the tower as a springboard tipped the balance and toppled the tower.

"As the brightly colored Sandboxes went flying, Buddy Basset took off on his short little legs and ran smack into the 100-gallon fish tank that the store had imported for the holidays. The fish tank flipped off its pedestal and crashed to the floor, spewing water and fish in all directions. Buddy suffered broken bones in three of his four legs and had to spend his first year of retirement being carted around in a wheelbarrow."

Havana paused to take a deep breath (and to allow Kat and Wolfe to get control of their laughter) before resuming. "Are you two ready for me to continue?"

Kat pressed her paws to her tiny mouth and nodded, as the last little giggle died in her throat. "Yes, Havana—forgive us. Please, go on."

"Okay. As soon the dust settled, the store manager got on the phone and called our corporate litigation department. I took the call and went out immediately. Oliver Wendell Hounds, the Associate General Counsel of our litigation department (and my boss), later assigned me to the case officially. But, I mean, I was there for the clean-up—literally. I got witness statements, talked to the cops who were called to the scene by Munchkin's hysterical parents. And later on, I deposed the doctors and the ambulance driver—"

"Deposed?" asked Wolfe.

"Oh, sorry. I took their depositions—interviewed them under oath."

"I knew that," said Wolfe, embarrassed by forgetting the simple term.

"Hey, no problem. Anyway, then the lawsuits started. Munchkin's parents sued us first, notwithstanding the fact that their precious little kitten didn't suffer so much as a bent whisker. Then Buddy Basset filed a personal injury claim against us. The Society for the Prevention of Cruelty to Fishes filed suit on behalf of the tank full of Goldfish guppies—most of which got eaten by those of our customers who didn't flee the store when the tower crashed. Finally, Sandboxes Incorporated filed suit against us for negligent infliction of slander—they made that up, but a judge out in California granted them leave to file—for $6 million in damages. There were also some random customer lawsuits that our insurance company settled quickly. I spent the next two years getting rid of the rest of the lawsuits—all except for Buddy's personal injury claim."

"How did you get rid of them?" asked Kat, an avid fan of Law & Order: Take 3000, now in its 215th iteration.

"Well, we counterclaimed against Munchkin for public nuisancy and assault with a loaded litterbox, and the parents agreed to drop their suit if we'd drop ours. The fish folks had limited funding and didn't pursue their case. And we filed a counterclaim against the Sandbox Company for negligent manufacturing."

"Negligent manufacturing?" asked Kat.

"Our theory of the case was that it was foreseeable that their product would be stacked for display and therefore, their failure to provide a stable stacking base was a proximate cause of the accident. . . . But, as it turned out, we didn't need the leverage. The Court granted my Motion to Dismiss their slander case."

"Why ?" said Kat.

"Well, the Judge asked them to explain, if Munchkin's accident 'slandered' the Company's reputation, how come Sandbox *hired* Munchkin to appear in a series of ads for the Super Sandbox. They couldn't."

"So, the only case left is Buddy Bassett's?" asked Kat.

"That's right," said Havana.

Wolfe looked puzzled. "Doesn't our insurance company usually handle *all* of these personal injury cases?"

"Generally they do," said Havana. "But only up to the damage cap. We self-insure against claims for damages in excess of $2 million. Since we have to pay anything over $2 million, we handle those cases in-house."

"What kind of damages is Buddy asking for?" said Wolfe.

"Fifty Million," replied Havana, as if it were pocket change. "The amount is outrageous, but let's face it, he makes a sympathetic plaintiff. He's a cute old guy. And he did have a lot of medical bills. The doctors decided Buddy would be better off if they fitted him with prostheses instead of trying to set the bones on his two left legs. You should see him scoot around on those little fake legs. He moves faster than he has in years."

"So how did you handle his lawsuit?" asked Kat, hoping that Havana was close to making her point.

"It was a tough negotiation, Kat. That's partly because Buddy is really mad at the company. He didn't want to retire and feels the company pushed him out the door. 'Like an unwanted piece of trash' is what he keeps whining. So he wants to make the company pay *something* out of its own pockets."

"You mean something more than the $2 million that the insurance company automatically pays," said Wolfe.

"Exactly. Anyway, after about a year of talks, we were finally starting to make progress when Buddy gets this book contract to write about his experience—<u>Four Legs to Nowhere</u>. The publisher gave him a huge advance, and he's been on all the talk shows. Shortly thereafter, the settlement talks stalled, and Buddy's lawyers are back to demanding the $50 million! I finally figured out what happened. It seems Buddy's publisher doesn't want him to settle. He figures there's another book in it, if the case goes to trial. I was at my wits end when I got lucky."

Wolfe grinned; "I'll bet you made your own luck, Havana."

"Well it helps to keep digging for more facts," smiled Havana. "One of the sales staff at the CatCo store suggested I talk with Vick Vendor. He's a retired CatCo salesdog who happened to be shopping in the store the day of the incident. He left before the accident occurred, but he had some very interesting information to share."

Havana leaned in conspiratorially.

"He told me it was well known among the sales staff that Buddy couldn't get through the day without his 'liquid help.' It seems Buddy carried a water bottle in his hip pocket that was filled with a little bit of water and a lot of Grey Goose. And most important, my witness not only *saw* Buddy sipping from his 'water' bottle that day, Vick took a sip when Buddy passed him the bottle, and he can testify that this particular mixture was something like 80 proof!"

Wolfe and Kat absorbed the significance of this information, as Havana laid it out

"If Buddy was drunk, his own actions were the proximate cause of his accident—not the negligence of the store and Feline Foods!"

"So the company was off the hook!" said Wolfe.

"It's never that clear-cut, Wolfe," Havana responded. "I figured if we went to trial, we'd still have an uphill battle, without any *tangible* evidence of Buddy's drinking. Plus, his lawyers could argue that even if Buddy *was* drinking, it didn't contribute to the accident.

"What Vendor's information *did* do however, is give me the bargaining chip I needed to negotiate a settlement. The roadblock was Buddy's publisher, so I figured that before the last settlement meeting, I would quietly suggest to him that the disclosure of Buddy's public drinking habits at trial would muddy his image and put a real damper on the sale of his book. With this new information, I judged that the best settlement we could possibly get them to agree to would be $4 million. Our insurance company would pay half, but the Company would still have to pay $2 million out of profits. I figured that should satisfy Buddy's desire to stick it to the company.

"Plus, I thought it was fair, considering the accident really was our fault—" Havana caught herself and quickly added, "I'll deny I ever said that!"

"At this point, I went to Oliver and got his okay to settle if I could get them to agree to $4 million."

Kat was anxious for Havana to get to the point. "Havana, it sounds like you did a great job on this case. What's the problem?"

Havana looked at Kat. Finally, she said, "I did do a great job, Kat. Then Oliver threw it all away . . . "

"What the heck happened?" demanded Wolfe.

"I'm not exactly sure," replied Havana. "But you can bet your last pipe of catnip that Cocker Spaniel had something to do with it!"

"Cocker Spaniel?" said Wolfe. "Is that the same canine who used to work for Dewey, Cheatum & Howe downtown?"

"Yes," said Havana, with an unpleasant smirk. "Oliver hired him about six months ago. His nickname is 'Cocky'—which is appropriate—but most of us think he should just leave off the 'y.'"

Wolfe laughed. He had met Cocky Spaniel, and he was, indeed, a real prick.

"A couple of weeks before the final settlement meeting, Oliver drops by my office with Cocky and tells me he's putting him on the Sandbox case team so he can get some experience 'working with one of our first-rate litigators.' I swear to you, that's what he told me. I guess I'm naïve; I actually believed him. So I took Mr. Cocker F. Spaniel under my wing, so to speak. Showed him everything we had on the case and even shared my negotiating strategy with him, since I agreed to let him attend that final settlement meeting. God, what a fool," she mumbled under her breath.

After a moment, Havana continued.

"When I walked into the settlement conference the following week, the first thing I see is *Oliver*, deep in conversation with Cocky. I have no idea what Oliver's even doing here, but before I can ask him, Bassett and his lawyer, Clancy Darrow, walk over and Oliver starts singing my praises. He tells

Clancy how he'd better 'run for cover' now that I'm here. Tells him I'm going to 'take 'em by the tails and cut of their . . . uh, you-know-whats! He says, 'Darrow, you'll be lucky if you can *walk* out of here with when Havana finishes with you.'"

"So he was there to support you?" asked Kat, still unsure where this was going.

"Maybe," said Havana, "but it was the worst thing he could do. He made it sound like I wanted to destroy them when my whole game plan was to create a win-win outcome. Oliver has this militaristic, scorched-earth approach to negotiating. I just don't work that way.

"The whole meeting was surreal. Oliver sat in the back and didn't open his mouth. Cocky sat at the table and participated as if he actually had a role! Every time I put a number out there, *Cocky* shot it down, saying we wouldn't pay a penny over $2 million! I had no idea what he was doing, but I quickly realized that Cocky's belligerence was the perfect foil to make my offer sound reasonable! And that's exactly what happened. Bassett's lawyers finally agreed to the $4 million offer and I accepted the deal. I looked for Oliver, but he was gone. . . . I guess that should have told me something . . . "

"I take it something happened after the meeting to 'un-settle' the agreement?" asked Kat.

"You could say that," said Havana. "The next day, Oliver calls me into his office and tells me that he's not sure he's satisfied with the terms of the settlement. I couldn't believe what I was hearing. I asked him, why? What terms didn't he like? He hemmed and hawed and never did give me an answer. Finally, he just said that it was his decision and that he'd made it. Oh! And *then* he tells me that he's already called Buddy's lawyers and rejected the agreement! I was so furious I couldn't even speak. I turned and left his office before I did anything I'd be sorry for.

"Anyway," Havana continued, "I knew Oliver's decision meant we'd be going to trial, so I figured I'd better put aside my anger and start getting ready. I spent every waking hour getting all of the background material in order, getting the depositions collected into trial notebooks, getting our witnesses in and preparing them . . ."

Havana's voice trailed off, like a toy that had wound down.

"Havana?" said Kat, and got no response. "Havana, what *happened*?"

Havana looked up. "Two weeks ago, I walked into my office and found Cocky standing at the conference table where I have all the trial documents laid out. He sees me and says, 'Hey, great job getting this stuff together, Havana. We're going to make a great team!'

"I'm thinking, damn it, Oliver's decided to let Cocky second chair my trial without even asking me."

Wolfe hated to interrupt, but he did: "Uh, 'second chair'?"

"Sorry," said Havana. "The lead counsel at trial is called the 'first chair.' The second chair is . . . whatever the first chair wants him to be. Generally, the second chair gets to haul the litigation bags to and from the courtroom," she concluded with venom.

"Would you like to guess what happened next?" Havana hissed. "Cocky looked at me and smiled—he actually *smiled* as he told me—he says, 'I'll want you to second chair this trial with me, of course!' 'I beg your pardon?!' I said to him, and he tells me that Oliver has assigned *him* to be the lead counsel at trial on <u>my</u> Sandbox case!!! I couldn't believe it. I *still* don't believe it."

Neither did Wolfe.

Oliver Wendell Hounds was in for a tough interview.

> *"* . . . talk to him in a language he under[stands]: the language of power.*"*
>
> *Found in the Historical Files, from Ancient Year 2006*
> *--Carly Fiorina, <u>Tough Choices</u>*

OLIVER "HOUNDS" HAVANA

Wolfe was furious! Havana was not just another cat who didn't get the big case. She was a friend; someone he'd worked with, admired, and liked. And *nobody* should be treated like that!

Kat was worried that Wolfe's personal feelings were going to color this next interview, but before she could say anything, the door to the conference room opened.

Oliver Wendell Hounds entered and sank into the nearest chair. His drooping jowls pulled his face into a long and weary frown. His tired eyes were rimmed in red and his dangling ears drooped onto the tabletop, the ends resting in folds on either side of his wrinkled forepaws.

Wolfe and Kat exchanged looks. She was glad to see the concern in Wolfe's eyes as they took in Mr. Hound's ancient appearance.

Kat offered him a bowl of water, which he graciously accepted, lapping up more than half of the water in one drink.

Having settled himself, Oliver Wendell Hounds looked up at Kat and then at Wolfe. "How can I help you?" he asked with a patrician dignity that belied his hangdog appearance.

"We want to talk with you about Havana Brown," said Kat.

"What do you want to know?" said Oliver, his expression blank.

Kat answered before Wolfe could vent his anger.

"We understand that Havana spent much of the last two years working on what she called the Sandbox case?" Kat began.

"Yes," said Oliver, "That's true. I think Havana did a good deal of the legwork on the case."

"So why the hell did you assign some two-bit lawdog to try the case instead of Havana?" growled Wolfe ignoring Kat's claws digging into his thigh.

Oliver stared at Wolfe, resentment evident in his craggy face.

Kat jumped in. "Mr. Hounds, please ignore Wolfe's tone. We're not here to challenge your decisions (glancing at Wolfe). We just want to understand how you make them."

Oliver took some time to remove his eyes from Wolfe. Finally he turned to Kat.

"Frankly, Ms. Woo, I don't understand why this has even come up. I gave the job to Mr. Spaniel because he *asked* for it. He's been asking me for an opportunity to try a case since the day he arrived here." Oliver appeared confused. "Is Ms. Brown upset about my decision?"

"Are you trying to tell us it didn't occur to you that Havana might be just a bit upset when you let someone else try her case after she did all the work on it?!" Wolfe blurted in frustration.

Oliver slowly processed this question.

"Actually, that didn't occur to me. .... I really didn't think she wanted the job."

Kat attempted to resume control of the interview. "So, you're saying that the attorney who works the investigative part of a case doesn't necessarily expect to become the trial attorney?"

Again, the three-second pause. "Well, it all depends. The original attorney may not have the experience to try the case, or they may have too much on their plate. There are many different factors that enter into my decision as to whom to assign as lead trial attorney."

"Well, Havana sure has just as much, *if not more,* experience than this Cocky character," grumbled Wolfe.

Oliver breathed deeply, exhaling with enough force to cause his ears to flap gently on the table.   "Havana *is* an experienced attorney, but she hasn't tried many cases.   And several months ago, when I asked her whom she thought should try the case if it went to court, she didn't seem interested."

"Are you saying you *asked* Havana to first-chair this case?" asked Wolfe, incredulously.

"You're not listening, Mr. Wolfe," replied Oliver. "I said that I asked Ms. Brown *who* should try the case.   Her response was that she 'wouldn't mind' trying the case herself . . . if I thought she was the best lawyer for the job."

"So she <u>did</u> ask for the case," said Wolfe.

Oliver stared at Wolfe. "I wouldn't call that 'asking' for anything, Mr. Wolfe. Trying a big case is something my lawyers fight over—not something I have to 'ask' them to do. I remember thinking at the time that she would be *happy* if I put someone else in charge."

Kat decided to change direction at this point.

"Mr. Hounds, let me ask you a different question. What do you actually think of Havana's skills as a lawyer? If she'd *asked* for the case, would you have given it to her?"

Oliver didn't answer right away.

"That's a bit of a circular question, Ms. Kat," he said finally. "The very fact that she didn't jump at the chance to try a big case actually made me wonder if she had the necessary confidence to be a good trial attorney." He paused, struggling with whether or not to continue.

"And there are other issues," he said at last. Oliver turned his mournful gaze toward Kat. "I want you to know that I really don't feel comfortable discussing this with you. I try never to say anything negative about any of my staff. But I assume you're going to insist."

"That's a wise assumption, Hounds," growled Wolfe. Kat kicked him.

"All right," said Oliver, his decision made. "You met with Havana this morning, is that correct?"

"Yes, just before you arrived," said Kat.

"Then perhaps you'll understand." He paused, then continued. "If you talked with Ms. Brown for any length of time, you know that she tends to spew forth words like bullets from an automatic weapon. You're never quite sure what direction they're going in; just as you start to follow one train of thought, she's off in a different direction. I find it tiring just trying to take in all the words, much less understand their meaning. Whatever comes into her head is sent straight to her mouth without any filter or organization. This 'stream of consciousness' communication is completely inappropriate for a litigator who must win over a jury. Trial lawyers must be consummate performers. They must be articulate and disciplined in making their case, slowly, meticulously, fact by fact. Trial work is a well-planned, organized, and disciplined communication."

"But don't you think she'd adopt a more professional style of speech in court?" asked Kat.

"Possibly," said Oliver. "But I've seen no indication of that. What I *have* observed is a style of talking that bespeaks mental chaos and causes me to question her competence."

"Her COMPETENCE?!?" Wolfe almost shouted. "Havana is one of the toughest, most *competent* cats I've ever worked with!"

Oliver's mournful face grew red and his watery eyes narrowed in anger. "You are not her boss, Wolfe. You are not responsible for her work. I am, and I don't want to be responsible for wasting two million dollars of this company's money!" The anger apparently exhausted Oliver, who appeared to deflate.

"Oliver, what two millions dollars are you talking about?" said Kat

"The Sandbox case settlement," he responded, sounding thoroughly worn out. "Havana wanted to settle with Buddy Bassett for $4 million. That offer was at least $2 million more than we needed to pay."

Kat started to speak, but Wolfe was louder. "You approved that settlement offer, yourself!" he barked. "And if you're so sure you could have settled for less, *why didn't you?* Aren't you costing the company at least that much and maybe more by going to trial?"

Oliver's face grew even redder and his breathing became labored. "I'm too old for this," he wheezed, as he started to rise. "I'm not going to sit here and be censured by this young pup. Not even Bernie has ever spoken to me like this."

Things were spinning out of control. Kat stood and put a gentle paw on Oliver's foreleg.

"Mr. Hounds—Oliver—I know this is hard on you, and I apologize. Please have a seat. I give you my word that we'll only be a few minutes—and that Wolfe won't open his mouth!"

Momentarily appeased, Oliver resumed his seat.

"Now," Kat resumed. "Can you just tell me what happened that caused you to lose confidence in Havana? If you'll tell us everything, I promise we won't interrupt."

Oliver began his story. "The first time I began to have doubts was when Havana asked me to approve her proposal to settle the case for $4 million. On paper, the $4 million didn't look like a bad deal for us—it's a far cry from the $50 million they'd asked for. But since I hadn't been involved in the negotiations, I needed Havana to assure me it was the best deal we could get. I don't recall her exact words, but she said something like 'I <u>think</u> it's the best we're going to do, and it <u>seems</u> like a fair offer.'

"What kind of an answer is that? She's supposed to get the <u>best</u> deal she can for Feline Foods – not what she thinks is 'fair.' And I don't want to hear that she 'thinks' it's a good offer.

I want her to tell me that it is absolutely the best deal we can get! How can I have confidence in the deal she's negotiated if *she* doesn't!?

"At that point, I decided I needed another pair of eyes taking a look at the deal. I asked Cocky Spaniel to get involved and give me his opinion on what the case was worth. And yes, I am aware that having one lawyer evaluate another will not provide the most reliable information . . . lawdogs are very competitive. That's why I went to the last settlement negotiation, myself. I wanted to see just how Havana was handling this thing."

Oliver paused for so long that, despite her promise, Kat spoke up. "How did that meeting go, Oliver?"

"Not well," Oliver replied immediately. "Not well at all.

"As soon as I arrived, Cocky approached me and said we shouldn't be offering more than $2 million—that's how much our insurance company would pay. He said Bassett wouldn't get half that much that if it went to trial. Then he told me why. Cocky told me that Havana had dug up some dirt on Mr. Bassett. Nothing that would put him in jail, mind you, but just bad enough to make him a very <u>un</u>sympathetic plaintiff—*and* make a big dent in the book sales of <u>Four Legs to Nowhere</u>.

"I was thrilled! I thought Havana would take this new information and cut our offer by half. I even boasted to Bassett's lawyer that Havana was going to bring them to their knees! . . . certainly shot *my* credibility all to hell!

"Near the end of that meeting, I was so embarrassed by Havana's performance that I left by the back door."

Oliver looked directly at Wolfe.

"Wolfe, I'd always had the same impression of Havana that you do—that she was brash, bold and tough! Well the lawyer I saw that day was none of those things. The only one in the room with any gumption was Cocky Spaniel! He really went after Bassett. Got in his face and said he'd only get a fraction of the money if he went to trial. And instead of supporting his efforts, Havana *used* him to negotiate a better deal for Bassett! She acted like a damned facilitator instead of Feline Foods' top litigator! I've seen tougher negotiators at a Tupperware party!!"

Oliver blushed, "I beg your pardon, Ms. Kat. Please forgive my language.

"The next day I called the Bassett hounds and told them we didn't have a deal. I had Cocky meet with them a couple more times to see if he could get them to settle for $2 million. When that didn't happen, I told him to take over the case and prepare for trial. He asked me if Havana could second-chair the case, and I told him that was his call.

"I don't know what your purpose is in asking me all these questions, but that's all I have to say."

"Oliver, thank you so much for sharing this information with us. Just one thing before you go," said Kat. "Have you spoken to Havana about any of this?"

"Spoken to her?" said Oliver. "You mean, told her what I just told you?" Kat nodded and Oliver continued. "Uh, no. . . I really didn't think that would be a good idea. I mean, I don't want to cause Havana any more upset. After all," he concluded, "it's not like she can change who she is, now, is it?"

"When decisions are made about promotion to management positions, the qualities sought are a high level of competence, decisiveness, and ability to lead. If it is [canines] . . . who are making the decisions about promotions . . . they are likely to misinterpret [feline's] ways of talking as showing indecisiveness, inability to assume authority, and even incompetence."

Found in the Historical Files, from Ancient Year 1994
by Deborah Tannen, Talking from 9 to 5

KAT & WOLFE TALK ABOUT 'TALKING'

Oliver left, and Wolfe sat staring into space.

Eventually, Kat said, "So. What are your thoughts about this morning?"

For the first time in their relationship, Wolfe did not respond with a quip. Clearly, the morning's meetings had troubled him.

"I don't know what to make of it, Kat. After we talked with Havana, I would have sworn that she'd been mistreated—and I still believe that. But after hearing Oliver's side of the story, I can understand why he was upset. He just didn't have enough information to understand Havana's negotiating strategy.

"Am I being unfair to Havana?" he asked,

"No, I don't think so, Wolfe. This is one of those perfect storms where nobody is wrong but everybody gets hurt. It's also an absolutely classic example of the kind of miscommunication that can happen when the participants are communicating in two different languages."

"You mean 'canine' and 'feline'?" asked Wolfe, with just the hint of a grin.

"You're learning, Wolfe," Kat replied, with a smile of her own. "There were at least three examples of miscommunication that wrecked havoc with the ability of Havana and Oliver to work successfully together. For example—"

"Wait—" said Wolfe. "Let me try. The first one's gotta be Havana's style of speaking. Oliver complained about that right out of the box."

"Exactly," said Kat. "Issue number one—let's call that the 'think-before-you-speak' issue."

Wolfe continued. "The next thing was the misunderstanding about whether Havana actually wanted to try the case or not. What Havana said and what Oliver heard were completely at odds."

"That's a big one. I call that the 'Ask for What You Want' issue," said Kat. "And the third?"

Wolfe thought about it. "I'm not sure what *caused* the problem, but somewhere along the line, Oliver started to question the way Havana was handling the negotiation and decided to get Cocky Spaniel involved to tell him what was going on."

"You're right," said Kat. "That issue is a little more complicated. Let's look at the other two issues, first."

Think Before You Speak

"As you noted, Wolfe, Oliver was not impressed with the way Havana conversed," Kat began.

"He sure wasn't," said Wolfe, recalling Oliver's comments. "What did he say? Something about her 'spitting out words like bullets'? What's so wrong with talking fast? I like fast-talkers; they waste less of my time!"

"Perhaps," replied Kat, "but you just put your paw on the problem. 'Fast talkers' are essentially saying 'I don't think what I'm saying is *worth* very much of your time.' Someone who speaks slowly and deliberately may be speaking gibberish – but that person conveys a strong degree of confidence in the value of his gibberish!

"And remember, speed wasn't the only issue," Kat continued. "Oliver also pointed out that Havana tends to jump from topic to topic in a random, stream-of-consciousness fashion, and he perceives this 'chaotic' conversation style as a measure of incompetence."

"But Havana *doesn't* jump from topic to topic," responded Wolfe. "She told us about the Sandbox case like a professional story-teller."

"True," said Kat. "That's because she'd been over the facts so many times her thoughts were well-organized before she spoke. With that kind of preparation, Havana can be eloquent."

"So why doesn't Oliver understand that*?*" Wolfe complained.

"Oliver judges her based on what he sees and hears. Since Havana doesn't filter her everyday conversations, Oliver sees the 'natural' Havana—the feline *we* heard when she first arrived. Havana's natural style of speaking is at lot like mine— she uses speech to flesh out ideas. That's okay if you're speaking to someone with the same style, who understands why you haven't finished a sentence in the last ten years. But Oliver may be a different personality type—someone who processes his thoughts internally and doesn't speak until his ideas are fully formed. To him, our natural style of speaking is unnerving, to say the least.

"So, what are you saying?" grumbled Wolfe. "That Havana has to change her natural way of speaking?"

"Yes and no. It's that two-part answer again, Wolfe: training and education. Both Havana and Oliver can be educated to understand that they process information differently. But that only opens the door to better communication. What happens next is up to Havana. If Oliver doesn't walk through that door to meet her halfway, she's the one who'll have to make changes."

"I can't believe I'm going to say this," said Wolfe, "but that doesn't seem very fair. I know, I know. I've complained that we canines are the ones who are always told we have to change, and I resent it. But I'm not sure that it should be only the felines who have to change, either. Shouldn't both groups have some responsibility?"

"That's the ideal, Wolfe. But I don't preach to the ideal. And frankly, there's a strong case that the responsibility for making sure real communication takes place belongs with the employee rather than the supervisor.

Curious, Wolfe asked, "Why?"

"Because an employee only has to communicate with <u>one</u> boss," Kat began.

" . . .whereas a boss might have a number of direct reports," Wolfe chimed in. "If he had to do the adapting, he might have to master four or five different styles."

"You catch on quick, Wolfe," Kat smiled. "Are all the Feline Foods executives this bright?"

"So, to summarize," said Wolfe, embarrassed by the compliment, "if Havana wants to grow her career under a boss whose style is substantially different from her own, she's the one who's going to have to make the effort."

Ask for What You Want

"Okay," said Kat. "Let's look at the next issue. "What was it Havana told Oliver when he asked her who should try the case? She 'wouldn't mind' provided he thought she was the best lawyer for the job? Let me ask you, Wolfe. How would you interpret that response?"

To his credit, Wolfe answered honestly. "It's hard for me to judge. I know Havana, and I know she'd jump at any chance to go to court. But I have to admit that her response to Oliver sure didn't express that enthusiasm, and it surprised the heck out of me." Wolfe looked perplexed. "Why would she hedge like that, Kat?"

"Because the biggest problem felines have is they don't know how to *ask for what they want!*" Kat was almost shouting. This was the first time Wolfe had seen such a visceral reaction from Kat. She continued speaking.

"Of all the feline training I do, Wolfe, this is the most difficult. So many felines are *terrible* at asking for what they want—*particularly* when they think they deserve it."

"Why, for heavens sake?" asked Wolfe.

"Fear, for one thing," replied Kat. "I don't think that was Havana's problem, but most of us have a natural fear of bosses. They have this life-and-death power over our careers. For cats, the fear is enhanced by a natural fear of canines as well as a more pronounced fear of rejection. If we ask, there's a chance the boss will say 'no.'"

"So what?" said Wolfe. "That just means you retool your argument and go back and ask again. What's so hard about that?"

"We speak a different language, Wolfe. When cats hear 'no,' most of us interpret it to mean 'absolutely not,' and 'you are a fool for thinking I would ever consider you!' Canines, as you just proved, interpret 'no' to mean 'not now,' or 'not this time' or even 'maybe.' So one hurdle for cats is be willing to *take the risk* and *ask*.

"But that leads into the next reason felines have such a problem with asking for what they want," Kat continued.

"What's that?" said Wolfe, clearly fascinated to learn how different the feline perspective really seemed to be.

"Asking for what you want, whether it's a choice assignment, more money, or a promotion, requires you to promote yourself. You have to tell your boss how good you are—why you deserve what you're asking for."

"Duh!" said Wolfe.

Kat assumed a wry grin. "It may be 'duh' to dogs, Wolfe, but felines for some unknown cultural reason are taught that it's unseemly to blow your own horn. There's a real disconnect between the way cats and dogs perceive the appropriate way to communicate one's accomplishments. Felines believe that their work speaks for itself. Frankly, we often get embarrassed by the 'shameless self-promotion' we hear from canines."

"That's just stupid!" said Wolfe. "How can they possibly expect a busy executive to know the details about everything his staff is doing—or how well they're doing it?"

Kat chuckled, but not with pleasure. "I can't disagree with you Wolfe. Nevertheless, we do. Whenever I make the suggestion that felines be more direct and more aggressive in asking for rewards, I *always* get a few who will argue that they 'shouldn't have to ask' because 'bosses should know' what they've done *and* should know what they want."

"That makes even less sense," said Wolfe. "How can we know what somebody's *thinking?* We're not—"

Wolfe was suddenly struck by a thought. "You know something, Kat? That's what my *wife* is always saying . . . She'll get upset; I'll say what's wrong; she'll says, 'You should *know* what's wrong!' Why on earth do felines think we're mind readers?!"

"Because by and large, felines *are* more perceptive than most canines," Kat admitted. "Plus, there's a good argument that *every* employee wants the obvious rewards of the workplace: good assignments, more money, and promotion—just like all students want A's. Felines reasonably assume these are things they shouldn't have to *ask* for, if their work is good enough."

"Yeah," said Wolfe. "I guess I can see that. But in school, *everybody* can get A's. At work, there are only so many openings and so much money. The boss *can't* give everybody everything they may deserve. It's 'the squeaky wheel that gets the grease,' right?"

"Well, that's a fairly gross way of putting it," grinned Kat. "But you're absolutely right. When I tell felines to 'manage their career', it's because that's what the canines are doing. The higher up you go, the more competition there is for fewer and fewer top jobs. Canines actively lobby their bosses for those jobs. If felines want to compete successfully, they've got to get in the game."

Manage Your Boss

"Okay," said Wolfe. "I'll buy that Havana should have been more conscious of her style of speaking when her boss was around, and she should have been more direct in asking for the assignment of lead attorney. But I think the whole settlement fiasco was caused by Cocky Spaniel's interference. That's not something you can blame on Havana."

"Wolfe, before we get into this issue, please, *please* stop thinking in terms of <u>blame</u>."

"Sorry, I didn't mean to say 'blame'—"

"The point is to identify ways that an employee can have more control over his or her own career—like monitoring her style of speech and learning to ask more directly."

"Okay, okay!" said Wolfe. "Sorry. It's just hard to think that way. But my original point is still valid. How do you stop someone like Cocky Spaniel from doing what he did?"

"You can't, Wolfe. There will always be 'Cocky Spaniels' in the workplace . . . peers or subordinates who go behind your back and attempt to undercut your position with your boss. I don't pretend to be able to stop that from happening. But there are ways to immunize yourself from such attacks. It's the first lesson in moving up the career ladder. Havana hasn't learned how to manage her boss. . . . she hasn't learned to 'manage up.'"

Suddenly, Wolfe's whole demeanor changed. "Wait a minute. Are you saying you want to come in here and teach cats how to manipulate their canine bosses? Kat, I've liked your approach so far, but I *don't* like the idea of being manipulated—and I know Bernie won't!"

"I said *manage,* Wolfe; not *manipulate,*" replied Kat. "But it's a fair question. The term has so much negative baggage that I hate having to use it. Let me share something with you."

Kat reached into her pawbag and pulled out a folder full of archive files. She handed one to Wolfe, and said, "Almost a thousand years ago, one of the greatest of all human universities published an article called *Managing Your Boss.* That article is still right on point, even in today's very different world. Take a look at what the authors say."

> *"To many people, the phrase 'managing your boss' may sound unusual or suspicious. Because of the traditional top-down emphasis in most organizations, it is not obvious why you need to manage relationships upward— unless, of course, you would do so for personal or political reasons. But we are not referring to political maneuvering or to apple polishing. We are using the term to mean the process of consciously working with your superior to obtain the best possible results for you, your boss, and the company."*
>
> --John J. Gabarro & John P. Kotter,
> "Best of HBR 1980: Managing Your Boss"
> HARVARD BUSINESS REVIEW, January 2005

Wolfe did not look convinced. "Well, they say one thing I agree with—it *still* isn't obvious to me why you need to 'manage' your boss."

"Actually, Wolfe, managing your boss has a lot to do with what we've just been talking about," said Kat. "It's the employee taking responsibility for learning how to communicate effectively with her boss. It's about understanding your boss— what his or her priorities are, how he/she likes to get information (in writing or in person), how much information he/she needs. . .. . .and using that knowledge to create a good working relationship built on trust."

Wolfe thought about what Kat had said for a few moments. "Look. I hear what you're saying, but how does it apply to the situation with Havana and Oliver . . . and Cocky."

"Okay," said Kat. "Let's look at what happened, here.

"First, let's acknowledge that Havana didn't take the time to get to know how much information Oliver needed to be comfortable with her work."

"How do you know that?" asked Wolfe.

"The first clue was Oliver's complete lack of knowledge about anything and everything Havana achieved over her two years work on the Sandbox case"

"Yeah," said Wolfe. "He did say something like he 'thought' she'd been involved in the case . . . I remember being surprised he didn't seem to know that she'd managed to settle most of the cases, already."

Kat continued. "She also failed to tell Oliver what she'd learned about Bassett's drinking habit or how she intended to use that fact in her negotiations—or even why she was sure Bassett wouldn't accept anything less than the $4 million offer. By not giving Oliver any background about what she was doing, Havana left herself wide open for someone like Cocky to undermine her efforts and curry favor with the boss."

"Okay," said Wolfe, "I agree with you about what happened. But I still don't see where Havana made a 'mistake,' so to speak. Most bosses *prefer* employees with initiative, who can take the ball and run with it. They don't *want* employees who constantly check with back with them for direction. . ."

"Checking back is one thing, Wolfe. *Informing* them is another. Hand me that article I just showed you," said Kat. She took it and flipped to page 29. "Here. Take a look at this. This article says bosses often want *more* information than their subordinates realize."

> *"How much information a boss needs about what a subordinate is doing will vary significantly depending on the boss's style . . .it is not uncommon for a boss to need more information than the subordinate would naturally supply or for the subordinate to think the boss knows more than he or she really does."*

Wolfe continued to look confused.

"Think of it like this," she suggested. "Suppose Rover wants to build a house. Rover hires Fluffy based on her reputation in the building community and tells her to design the biggest house possible on his acre of land. Fluffy takes into account all the setbacks, the septic field requirements, height restrictions and soil compaction and designs the biggest house that the land will accommodate. She shows him the plans. He says, is this the biggest house I can build?

"What should she say in reply? The very fact that Rover asks the question means he has some doubts. Fluffy doesn't know what his underlying concerns are, but she needs to build up his confidence in her and her plans. So her answer is to give him as much information about the design as he will listen to. She needs to tell him *why* the house can't be taller, wider, or longer and answer any questions he may have."

"But isn't that a waste of time?" insisted Wolfe. "Rover doesn't know anything about house-building and isn't going to understand the engineering involved. That's why he hired an expert. Besides, he's already hired her to do the job."

"Maybe. But that doesn't mean he can't change his mind. Rover may do exactly what Oliver did: get a second opinion," replied Kat. "Suppose Rover asks another architect if Fluffy's plan really gives him the biggest house possible. The new architect is Fluffy's competitor – he wants Rover's business and he's now in a position to get it. All he has to do is tell Rover the house *can* be bigger and find some way to explain why. Even if his explanation is bogus, he's undermined Fluffy's credibility just by telling Rover what he wants to hear and backing it up with an explanation – something he doesn't have from Fluffy!"

Wolfe began to grin. "So telling your boss why you're doing something that may not be exactly what he'd hoped for. Its like an effort to CYA—that's Cover You're As—"

"I KNOW what it means, Wolfe," Kat said. "I'd prefer to think of it as making your boss *comfortable*—comfortable with you. Comfortable that you're going to give him all the information he needs to know so that he can *defend* whatever you're doing, should the need arise. The best employees will figure out how much information the boss needs, how he wants it communicated, what his priorities are, etc. That's what managing your boss is all about. It is the most sophisticated of all of the career management skills I teach."

"I'm looking forward to your 'lessons' for Havana," said Wolfe, with a smile.

"The conversations in which you ask your boss for something are important to your career. . . . Managing up is the groundwork you do before you start one of these important conversations."

Found in the Historical Files, from Ancient Year 2007 by Penelope Trunk, Brazen Careerist: The New Rules for Success

L essons for Havana

I. THINK BEFORE YOU SPEAK

Why?

> *"Conversations at work can be, in a sense, like a test. What we say as we do our work can become evidence on which we are judged, and the judgments may surface in the form of raises (or denials of raises), promotions (or their lack or their opposite), and favorable (or unfavorable) work assignments."*
>
> <u>Talking from 9 to 5</u>. (pg. 12-13)

Havana has already made it into the upper levels of the corporate hierarchy, as a professional. She is reasonably sophisticated about the politics of the workplace, and will probably have no difficulty understanding *why* her style of speech could be causing communication problems with Oliver. Nevertheless, she should read Deborah Tannen's <u>Talking from 9 to 5</u>. It's the most definitive work on the entire topic of male/female communication in the workplace. One of the book's reviewers called it the "Rosetta stone that at last deciphers the miscommunication between the sexes."

How?

Modifying the way in which you converse with others in the workplace can be challenging. Deborah Tannen notes that

> *"we can't just tell individuals that they should simply talk one way or another, as if ways of talking were hats you can put on when you enter an office and take off when you leave."* (*Talking from 9 to* 5, p. 34)

Nonetheless, there are certain things Havana can do that will enhance her ability to communicate with her boss as well as improve her overall image as a leader.

1. *Slow down.* Havana's enthusiasm is embodied in the speed with which she speaks and she doesn't have to give that up completely. She can begin by deciding when it is most important to speak more slowly, and concentrate her efforts to 'slow down' on those specific occasions.

Initially she might just focus on her speed when talking with her boss. Since Oliver's speech is slow and ponderous, Havana can concentrate on mirroring his speed.

Like all new behaviors, the "secret" to incorporating it into your natural habits is practice, practice, practice. Get a tape recorder and record yourself giving a speech or discussing an issue. Then listen to yourself. Make notes of what you like and what you want to improve. Then re-record the speech. Do this until you like what you hear.

Another way to master the speed of your speech is to time yourself. According to author Phyllis Mindell, in <u>A Woman's Guide to the Language of Success</u>, you should deliver between 100 and 125 words per minute. This includes time for appropriate pauses. Select a speech to practice with, count the words, and clock yourself as you speak it out loud. The very process of timing your speech will help to develop your sensitivity to the speed at which you talk. Practice until you always reach the one minute mark within the 100-125 range. Then practice until you can hit the 100 mark or the 125 mark, at will.

> "Sandra Day O'Connor, the first woman to be named to the Supreme Court, was asked shortly after her appointment what problems she had encountered on her way up the legal ladder. She replied that getting men to listen remained a continuing challenge. 'I taught myself early on to speak very slowly—enunciating every word—when I wanted someone's undivided attention.'"
>
> from an article by Patricia O'Brien in <u>Working Woman,</u> Feb. 1993;
> Reprinted in <u>A Woman's Guide to the Language of Success</u>, p.103

2.   *Filter your speech.* Felines have a tendency to believe that persuasion depends upon the number of facts you provide to support your point. While this may be true in a courtroom trial or a formal debate, it is not generally true in the workplace. Bosses don't have the time to absorb all of the details needed to make the decision from scratch. That's why they have *you*. If the boss knows that *you* have confidence in what you're telling him, he will trust that you have adequately researched and analyzed the details.

Deborah Tannen writes of a CEO who spent much of his day hearing short presentations about action issues that require his 'go or no go' decision.

> *"He has to make a judgment in five minutes about issues*
> *that presenters have worked on for months. 'I decide,' he*

explained, 'based on how confident they seem. If they seem very confident, I call it a go. If they seem unsure, I figure it's too risky and nix it.'"　　　　　*(Talking from 9 to 5, p. 34)*

When Havana talks with Oliver, it will be important for her to think about what she wants to say in advance and summarize the important points. Initially, she may want to write out a short summary to keep on track.

Another way to filter your speech is to take the advice lawyers always give when preparing witnesses for cross-examination—count to three before you answer any question. This prevents you from blurting out the first thing that comes into your head (which could lead into a tangential topic you really didn't want to discuss) and gives you time to frame an articulate answer.

II.　　ASK FOR WHAT YOU WANT

Why?

> "Career consultants see ...an epidemic among professional women: The tendency to work hard, assuming they will be rewarded. Studies consistently show that one reason for the compensation discrepancy between men and women is three little words: Women don't ask. To paraphrase the line from the movie *Cool Hand Luke*, 'What we have here is a failure to negotiate.'"
>
> Martha A. Woodham, *"How do you get what you want?"*
> Pink *Magazine, Aug/Sept 2006, p. 64*

Asking for what you want in the workplace is difficult because it generally requires you to justify your request – to answer the unspoken question, 'Why are you worth it?' And *that* means promoting yourself.

The concept of self-promotion is fraught with negative imagery: brag, boast, crow, show off, sing your own praises, talk big, blow your own horn. Who in their right mind would want to engage in any of these horrid practices? Females, in particular, are trained from a very young age to be modest and are told that if you do a good job, people will notice you.

That works—until you find yourself in competition with someone who isn't sitting back and hoping to be 'noticed.' If your competition knows how to make himself (or herself) sound like the Lamborghini of employees, not only will the boss want him, he'll pay more to get him.

How?

Unlike the many felines who think they shouldn't have to tout their accomplishments or ask for what they want, Havana understands the rationale. What she needs to learn is how to ask and boast *effectively.*

One of the first things Havana might do is read <u>Brag: The Art of Tooting Your Own Horn Without Blowing It</u> by Peggy Klaus. It provides an in-depth look at what prevents so many of us from tooting our own horn, and offers a number of ideas for becoming an effective self-promoter.

The first requirement is understanding the importance of crafting the *right message.*

> "Self-promotion is all abut the *quality* of one's message and story, rather than a boring list of accomplishments."
>
> <u>*Brag!*</u> *p. 14*

The Artful Boast

Here are a few guidelines for creating the perfect blend of humility and self-promotion that makes an Artful Boast.

1.   *Use Specific Examples*!   Sit down and make a list of your personal accomplishments.   Be sure to list the key facts that made you successful.   Here are different approaches Havana might have taken.

Weak:

I've resolved a number of cases.

Artful:

I was able to get three of the cases dismissed, Oliver. And the settlement I got the final plaintiff to agree to will save the Company considerable money compared with going to trial.

---

2.   *Connections.* Try to frame your accomplishments in ways that are relevant to your listener.

Weak:

I've done a great job in the negotiations, Oliver.

Artful:

Buddy Bassett's lawyers were impressed with how I handled the negotiations, Oliver – they said you must be a great mentor.

---

3.   *Authenticity.*   A key to selling anything—yourself included—is to project a genuine enthusiasm for the 'product.' Perversely, efforts to promote ourselves often make us uncomfortable . . . which tends to destroy any semblance of sincerity.

The only way to avoid this vicious circle is to practice until you are comfortable with what you have to say. Remember, it's fine to be enthusiastic about yourself and your abilities. If you aren't, who will be?

4.   *Humor* is the most valuable tool in your verbal toolbox. We're not talking about sarcasm or any other form of 'humor' that belittles others or even yourself. But mild self-deprecation is appropriate in an Artful Boast as a counterbalance to appearing too smug. Notice how the author of *Brag!* "brags" that

> "I . . . have been invited to academia to torture those poor souls at Wharton and UC Berkeley's Haas MBA programs."
>
> *Brag!* p. 45

she has been invited to speak to the MBA students at Wharton and Berkeley, then gently pokes fun at herself by saying she was invited to "torture those poor souls."

The Formula.

Now that you have the elements of an Artful Boast, the next step is putting them together.. In the beginning, try using the following simple formula for creating your Artful Boasts:

FRAME—BOAST—TEMPER—BOAST—WHAT'S NEXT

The statement in the box below is an example of what Havana might have said to Oliver to promote the fact that she successfully got one of the earlier lawsuits in the Sandbox Case dismissed. See how each part fits into the formula for creating the Artful Boast.

> Oliver, have you got a minute? I thought you'd like to know that I got Sandbox, Inc. to agree to dismiss their lawsuit against us. Of course, their suit had no merit whatsoever, but Sandbox has a lot of money and a large team of lawyers and could have wasted a lot of Feline Foods' time and money. We're meeting next week to sign the agreement.

Frame: *Oliver, have you got a minute?*	When phoning or dropping by the boss's office, it is critical to give the boss an opportunity to say he's busy; otherwise, not only will he be annoyed at being interrupted, he won't be listening to what you're saying
Boast: *I thought you'd like to know that I got Sandbox to agree to dismiss their lawsuit*	Havana is informing her boss that she accomplished an important goal— getting a lawsuit dismissed.
Temper: *Of course, their suit had no merit whatsoever, . . .*	Havana 'tempers' her achievement by noting that their suit was frivolous. (Note that this does not unduly lessen her 'credit' since even frivolous lawsuits are costly to defend against.)
Boast: *. . . but Sandbox has a lot of money and a large team of lawyers and could have wasted a lot of Feline Foods' time and money.*	Here, Havana is pointing out that she has saved the Company a lot of money, *specifically* noting that the plaintiff corporation had the means to pursue an expensive trial.
What's Next: *We're meeting next week to sign the agreement*	Finally, Havana notes when and how the deal will be completed.

Another way to "temper" your boast is to thank or credit others. For example, in "boasting" about your promotion, it's artful to thank your current team for their great work and credit them with being partly responsible for your getting the promotion.

A third way to "temper" your boast is through humor.

Do It!

You are now ready to create your own Artful Boasts. A good way to begin is to draft a personal 30-second "elevator introduction." This is what you wish you had told the CEO of your company about yourself that day when you and he rode the elevator together to the 23rd floor!

Next, create an Artful Boast that chronicles the most recent achievement you haven't told your boss about. When you're finished, *tell your boss!* Get over the idea that 'the less I bother my boss, the better and stronger I look.' Instead, think 'out of sight; out of mind' – and go be 'seen' by your boss.

How should you keep your boss informed? Regular meetings? Send a written weekly report? Use email? Just drop in on your boss?

You'll know the answer to that when you, like Havana, have become adept at "managing up!"

III.   Manage Up

Why?

> "The goal of managing up is not currying favor. . . . it's becoming more effective."
>
> Liz Simpson, "Why Managing Up Matters"
> *Harvard Management Update*, August 2002.

128

Your "boss" as your " client." The term "managing up" or "managing your boss" are inelegant descriptions of the process of developing an effective working relationship with your boss. To understand why it makes sense that this task is primarily *your* responsibility, reframe the relationship. Instead of thinking of your boss as your *employer*, think of him as your *client.* Both employers and clients hire you to perform work for them. Yet we tend to pay far more attention to the needs of our client than we do to the needs of our boss.

Developing such a relationship delivers the best possible results for your company, as well as for both you and your boss.

How?

What do you need to learn about your boss? Here are some of the things you should think about:
- What are his objectives
- What are his strengths and weaknesses
- How does he like to get information: memos, meetings, emails, phone calls?
- Does he appreciate conflict or try to avoid it?
- Is he a high-involvement manager or does he prefer a hands-off style
- Style of decision-making: in group discussion or afterward, by himself.

Many felines tend to take job descriptions at face value and assume to know what needs to be done. Without realizing it, they are setting their own priorities. You will be far more successful (and happier) if you make an effort to determine your boss's specific objectives and work on those.

"'Forty percent of my clients tend not to be aware of their boss's needs. . . .There's a vague notion that they're just not clicking but they're not able to articulate why. I ask them to clarify their top five responsibilities with their boss so that both understand and agree on what those priorities are. That's a conversation everyone needs to have.'"

Liz Simpson, "Why Managing Up Matters," quoting Relly Nadler
Harvard Management Update, August 2002.

There are no "secrets" to learning about your boss, other than to ASK. Sometimes, you can ask someone other than your boss, such as peers who've been working with him successfully. Or ask his secretary, who knows the most, appreciates being asked, and is generally happy to help.

Bosses are not necessarily able to answer all of these questions directly. Some things you'll have to learn by paying attention.

"Managers who work effectively with their bosses. . .seek out information about the boss's goals and problems and pressures. They are alert for opportunities to question the boss and others around him or her to test their assumptions. They pay attention to clues in the boss's behavior."

John Gabarro & John Kotter, "Managing Your Boss"
Harvard Business Review, Jan. 2005.

Finally, once you've identified your boss's objectives and management style, you need to accommodate yourself to that style. That doesn't mean you must become something you're not; no one can do that effectively. But you can adapt to the boss's conversational and managerial styles often without changing anything important to you.

For example, if your boss hates email—*don't send him email updates!* On the other hand, the *fact* that your boss hates email may be a crucial piece of information for an alert employee. Today, very few workplaces function without a significant reliance on email. If email is one of your boss's 'weaknesses,' see if there is some way you can *help* your boss accommodate to the new technological workplace. Don't wait for him to ask; he may never think about it. Come up with an idea and volunteer your help. Even if it doesn't work out, your boss will appreciate your initiative.

Remember, the time you spend establishing a good working relationship with your boss is an investment in your future. Much of what you need to do is a one-time effort. *Establishing* the relationship can take a good deal of time and effort; *maintaining* it takes just a little time and much less effort.

CAREER MANAGEMENT 301:
"THE PEAK YEARS"

Career Tips – Speak the Language

Think Before You Speak

- Adapt your style of conversation to your boss

- Business talk is *always* different from personal talk; deliver your message clearly and concisely

- Avoid modifiers and hedges that 'minimize' your words

- In meetings, speak EARLY, speak UP, and speak OFTEN (but not *too* often)

- Slow your speech to gain and keep your audience's attention

Ask for What You Want

- You don't get what you don't ask for

- Never assume your boss knows what you want – ASK for it!

- "No" usually means "ask again, later"

- *Practice* your 'ask' out loud

- Only your mother can read your mind

Learn to Manage UP

- Career success is successfully managing the relationship with your boss

- Cultivate a productive working relationship by spending time with the boss; "face time" isn't just cosmetic

- Learn your boss's strengths, weaknesses, priorities, and work style

Part 5:
Play to Win

"When men interact, they are always evaluating the level of competence of others.

"Yet competence is not enough. . . Power in the workplace does not only involve competence, but even more important is the perception of power.

"On Mars, the perception of power earns the greatest respect."

Found in the Historical Files, from Ancient Year 2002
John Gray, Mars and Venus in the Workplace

THE PURRFECT CAT

Zoë Katz opened the door to the conference room and paused in the entranceway. She smiled at Wolfe.

Zoë was a full Turkish Angora, as purebred a feline as Kat had ever seen. Her stark white coat shimmered in the light of the morning sun that shown through the southeast window in the small conference room. Large, almond-shaped eyes of deepest emerald green turned to Kat with an open, intelligent expression.

"I'm Zoë Katz," she said in a warm, well-modulated purr. "You must be Kat," she continued, extending her long tapered forepaw. "Bernie has told me such wonderful things about you."

Kat took the offered paw. "Thank you, Zoë; that's always nice to hear."

Zoë turned to Wolfe. "And you're Ryan Wolfhound. I haven't had the opportunity to meet you."

Kat watched Zoë converse with Wolfe. From the moment this extraordinary feline had appeared in the doorway, it was obvious that Zoë Katz was someone special. She exuded the charisma of leadership. Zoë could be the poster cat for feline CEOs. Zoë's career to date matched well with Kat's initial impression—almost. Top in her class at Harvard Business School, she had been hired directly into sales management. Working with more and bigger clients, her success had earned her promotion to regional management. Five year ago, she had been promoted to one of the two Vice Presidents of Brand Management, with responsibility for the sales and marketing of the Company's Economy Brands. Under Zoë's leadership, the Economy Brands, while targeted to the lower end of the market, produced a larger portion of the Company's revenue than the more prestigious Premium Brands.

This made it all the more puzzling as to why Zoë had been passed over twice for promotion to the position of Senior Vice President of Brands. Kat suddenly began to worry; what if this was a case of discatination. How would Bernie react to *that* conclusion?

Her reverie was interrupted by the sound of Wolfe's gruff laughter responding to something Zoë had said.

Kat smiled with pleasure as she noticed how effectively Zoë had engaged Wolfe. "We should probably get started," she said.

After they were seated, Kat began. "Zoë, I believe you are aware of why we asked to talk with you?"

"As I understand it," replied Zoë, "you've been asked to resolve the Company's concern as to why so few felines are promoted into the ranks of top executives." As an afterthought, she added, "And I am encouraged to talk freely because these conversations are to be completely confidential."

"Well put," smiled Wolfe, clearly charmed. Kat could not repress a grin at Wolfe's reaction to Zoë. It wasn't sexual—at least, not in the ordinary sense of the word. Zoë's beauty was understated rather than focused, but it was nonetheless overwhelming. Much of it was the way she carried herself; she stood tall, stretched to her full height by the lift of her head and the straight set of her shoulders. Her voice was soft – at odds with the stereotypical deep bark of leadership. But it was low, and she spoke slowly and with a clarity that wrapped her words in confidence.

Zoë continued speaking. "Kat, I really don't know what I can tell you. Overall, I've been lucky." Her eyes somehow managed to convey absolute sincerity while at the same time hinting at unspoken thoughts.

Kat frowned down at the file on the table before her. "That may be," she said "but I have trouble understanding why someone of your caliber was passed over twice for a promotion to head Brand Management."

Wolfe winced visibly at Kat's blunt statement, but Zoë's face remained a mask of polite interest. "All I can tell you, Kat, is that I have continued to be reviewed and rewarded at the top of the pay scale—both in salary and bonuses. At the high end of the corporate ladder, competition for promotions is fierce, and judgments are very difficult. I can't fault the Company's decisions."

"You think the dogs who were promoted were more deserving?" Kat challenged.

"Of course not," Zoë said evenly. "If I didn't think I was the best Brand Marketing executive in the Company, I wouldn't be worth the salary they are paying me." Zoë paused, then continued, somewhat reluctantly. "Actually, the first time the

Senior VP job came open, I wasn't even in the running. I had only been in my job for eight months. The canine they promoted had been a Brand VP for 15 years.

Wolfe jumped in. "That would have been Max, right? Max. . . what was his last name?"

"Moocher," said Zoë, helpfully.

"That's right!" Wolfe said happily. "Maxwell X. Moocher. What a character! He didn't do very well in the three-plus years he was in that position, as I recall," Wolfe continued, looking at Zoë apparently hoping that she would jump in and agree.

Zoë remained silent.

Kat resumed. "All right. Seniority is a valid, if not always a good, criteria for promotion. By the way, who got Max's job when he moved up?"

Zoë's vivid green eyes became shuttered, as she realized where Kat was going with this question. She had no choice but to answer, however. "Dwight replaced Max," she said. "Dwight W. Knight."

Kat looked at the file, pretending to read, then looked up. "Dwight W. Knight?" she said feigning surprise. "Isn't that the dog they just promoted to run the Brand Marketing Department? Didn't he have less time on the job than you did?" Kat paused. "I guess seniority wasn't as important this time," she finished.

Wolfe was ready to kill Kat and probably would have if he hadn't understood the point of her sharp-edged questions. In fact, he was becoming almost angry at Zoë for her seeming complacency. She clearly deserved promotion. Why wasn't she angry about it? Why wasn't she arguing her case?

Zoë seemed to withdraw within herself. She made no move, but the openness that was apparent when she'd first arrived had disappeared, replaced by a blank politeness that gave no clue to what was going on behind the closed expression.

"Kat, I appreciate what you are doing—what the Company is trying to do. But Texas Rex's decision to promote Dwight had nothing to do with me. It was a matter of circumstances. Canines tend to be quite impressed by a manager's ability to deal with crises. Dwight faced a major crisis just before the promotion decisions, and he handled it masterfully. It was not unfair to reward him."

Wolfe noticed that as she spoke, Zoe looked directly at Kat and some kind of understanding seemed to pass between the two felines.

After a moment, Kat said to Zoe, "I see. It's hard to compete against a crisis-killer when you don't experience a crisis, isn't it.

"Quite difficult," replied Zoe.

Wolfe knew there was more being said here than he understood, but it was clear the interview was over, and Wolfe was hungry. So he brought things to a close.

"Zoe, thanks for coming and for being straight with us."

"Yes, thank you," echoed Kat. "I enjoyed meeting you. I hope we'll have an opportunity to get better acquainted. Let's have lunch sometime."

"How about tomorrow?" Zoë replied.

"I'd love to," said Kat.

Wolfe adopted a hurt puppy expression. "What's this?" he asked, "the 'Old Girl's Network'? Canines are dogma non gratis?"

"That's right," Zoë laughed.

"Maybe next time," said Kat.

Ever the competitor, Wolfe conveniently recalled that he had "a lunch meeting with Bernie," for the following day.

> "But the proof of her competence was invisible: the *absence* of errors. How do you get your bosses to see something that did not happen?"
>
> *Found in the Historical Files, from Ancient Year 2007*
> *Deborah Tannen, Talking from 9 to 5*

TEX AND THE STORY OF 'REGULATION G'

"Texas Rex" was perhaps the biggest canine Kat had ever seen. A mastiff weighing almost 200 pounds, he filled the room not only with his bulk but with his hearty manner and his booming Texas drawl. It was these characteristics that had made Tex the most successful salesdog in the Company's history. There was just something that customers *liked* about Tex. If he hadn't been making so much money in sales, he would have been a great politician—as several former Presidents had suggested, and as he liked to tell folks whenever the opportunity arose.

The two big dogs greeted each other in typical fashion, adopting a fierce pose and growling as if prepared to fight to the death. Wolfe broke the moment first and poked Tex gently on his massive shoulder. "Great to see you, Tex. It's been a while. When are you going to invite me out to that ranch of yours for some hunting?"

"As soon as you learn *how* to hunt," Tex teased, turning to Kat.

Wolfe looked ready to prolong the repartee, but realized that Tex wanted to be introduced to Kat. "Tex, this is Kathryn

Woo, our Canine/Feline Resource consultant. Ms. Woo, this is Texas Rex, Executive Vice President of Sales and Marketing for the Company—"

"—and the best durn salesdog this Company's ever seen." Tex added. "Never did figure out why Bernie went and made me an executive." Tex pronounced it 'execative' as he did whenever he determined that his Texas twang would be useful. This was generally in conversations with customers—and with cats he found attractive.

"I can't imagine," said Kat, annoyed to realize that Tex did not take her or this meeting seriously.

Tex gazed intently at Kat, trying to determine if he had just been insulted. Before Tex could respond, however, Kat continued, "Can we get started, Mr. Rex? I know your time is very valuable."

This time, Tex looked at Wolfe, who shrugged his shoulders and tried hard not to laugh.

Tex settled down in the big chair at the end of the table, and stretched his huge fore paws out in front of him.

"All right, Ms. Woo," he responded, with no trace of a drawl. "How can I help you?"

Suddenly, Kat realized the raw power in the corporate version of this canine and wished for a moment that she had not chased away the friendly Texas cowboy.

She thought it prudent to make a gesture of appeasement, so she said, "Please feel free to call me Kat." When he failed to return the offer to call him by his first name, she quickly continued. "What we'd like to know is what factors prompted you to promote Dwight Knight to the position of

Senior Vice President of Brand Marketing and Management rather than Zoë Katz."

Tex gave Wolfe a sharp look. "I'm not accustomed to having my decisions second-guessed, Wolfe," he said.

Kat signaled Wolfe to let her handle this, and he readily complied.

"Mr. Rex," she said politely, "I am not here to *challenge* your decision; I am here to *defend* it."

Tex's eyebrows shot up so fast, Kat thought they might take leave of his head.

"Honey," he barked in a loud voice, the Texas twang sneaking back into his speech, "I'm a salesman, and I know when someone's spreadin' a load of horse manure—and that's the biggest load o' crap I've heard since the Democats left office! In fact, you're here to show us dogs that we're a bunch of cat-chasin' chauvinists!"

"Nonsense," said Kat said with a twinkle in her voice. "Why on earth would Bernie pay good money to teach you anything so obvious ?" Kat held her breath.

Tex looked thunderous for a moment, and then suddenly, he broke into peels of raucous laughter that brought tears to his eyes. "Damn, girl. You're pretty sharp for a little thing," he said as he wiped his eyes. Tex took a deep breath and said, "Okay, Ms. Woo—Kat—you win. I'll tell you what I can. . . . And, call me Tex."

"Thank you, Tex," said Kat. "Now, about the promotion?"

Tex leaned back in his chair and began.

"I thought about it," said Tex, and Kat could hear the sincerity in his voice. "You know, Kat, I really like Zoë. She's a great cat—and she's great at her job. Believe me, I really wanted to be able to move a feline into the executive ranks. We need to do more of that."

"But. . ." prompted Kat.

"But *this* time, there really wasn't any decision to make—the choice was obvious. Dwight pulled off a dad-burned miracle! He saved the Company a couple million dollars. There's no way he didn't deserve that promotion."

Wolfe looked satisfied.

Kat was silent for a moment as she looked at Tex. "Can you tell me what he did?"

"Sure can," smiled Tex, who leaned forward, relishing the opportunity to tell Dwight's story—to tell any story, for that matter. Tex was a born raconteur.

"It all started early last year, when some fool government *(Tex deliberately pronounced the word "gumint")* scientist –"

Wolfe broke in with the totally gratuitous comment that "Tex is not a fan of the government."

"Yes, I can see that," said Kat.

Tex continued as if uninterrupted. "This so-called scientist with nothin' better to do and more money than sense says he's discovered this new vitamin that's crucial to the diet of the entire feline population. Called the thing 'Kormien'."

"Named it after himself," added Wolfe.

"*And*, he convinced the folks down in 'Washington Dee Cee' that every brand of premium cat food ought to provide at least 50% of an adult cat's need for this stuff."

"It must have cost the Company an arm and a leg to comply with something like that!" said Kat in astonishment.

"Actually, the *law* didn't cost us a penny!" crowed Tex. "Our Regs&Rules department did some tests and learned that *all* of our brands had plenty of this Kormien in 'em."

Kat looked puzzled. "Then what caused the 'crisis'?"

"Well, Ma'am," continued Tex, spinning the story like a ball of fine twine, "it seems that just havin' a law is never good enough for the government. No, they have to have 'regulations' to go along with the law, in case anybody actually *understood* the law, ya see. So the regulators went about regulating and ended up with hundreds of pages of useless nonsense that went into effect as of January 1 of this year—3003. And somewhere in those hundreds of pages of regulations, was this *Regulation G*."

"And '*Regulation G*' said what?" asked Kat, drawn into the tale in part because of her interest and in part by Tex's natural story-telling ability.

"*Regulation G* said that every package of cat food had to have a special message printed on the label tellin' folks about the wonders of Kormien and letting everybody know just how much Kormien that package contained. And *Regulation G* required that this message be on every label shipped after January 1, 3003." Tex paused for effect. Then he continued.

"On January 15th, we shipped a $10 million order of Feline Premium Plus to Feelgood Foods—one of our biggest customers. When it arrived at the loading dock, they refused to accept it."

"Because it didn't have the label?" Kat ventured.

"Precisely!" said Wolfe, anxious to show Kat that he knew the inside story.

"But why not?" asked Kat, turning to Tex.. "Doesn't a Company of this size have someone who monitors changes is the law?"

Tex looked momentarily annoyed at the interruptions. Nonetheless, he responded: "We've got a whole *Department* of Governmental and Regulatory Affairs. But apparently they've got more 'important' things to do than let Sales & Marketing know that a new law is going to mean we have to change the packaging design of every food product we sell."

Kat could see the anger sparking in Tex's big brown eyes and thought it best to get him back to the story of Dwight's coup.

"So, what happened?" she asked. "Did the trucks have to turn around and bring the $10 million shipment back here?"

"No way," Tex boomed with pride. "Fortunately, Dwight got the news before the trucks left. He told them to wait there and he'd see what he could do. I'm tellin' you, when that pup sets his mind to it, I don't think there's anything he can't get done! Dwight got on that telephone and talked to more important people in an hour than most of us meet in a lifetime. He got hold of Senator Daschelhound, one of the most powerful Senators in Congress—"

("Who has a lot of stock in Feline Foods," added Wolfe, helpfully.)

"and got the Senator to put some pressure on the Secretary of Agriculture—"

("Who's married to Bernie's sister," added Wolfe.)

". . . to get the FFDA Commissioner—"

("Who ran the manufacturing operations at Feline Foods for 15 years.")

". . .to issue an executive directive granting an extension for compliance with *Regulation G* to all cat food companies with revenues in excess of $10 billion!" concluded Tex.

Wolfe added his final sidebar.

"Which *only* applies to Feline Foods."

Tex looked at Kat triumphantly. "Now *that's* leadership," he said with conviction.

"Yes," Kat agreed, thoughtfully. "Dwight certainly came through in the crisis."

After a moment or two, Kat looked at Tex and asked, "If Dwight hadn't been in the picture, can I assume you would have promoted Zoë?"

Texas Rex didn't even hesitate. "You betcha," he answered. "That cat has it all."

Kat smiled from ear to ear.

KAT & WOLFE TALK ABOUT WINNING

Wolfe looked at Kat and grinned. "I don't know about you, but I sure can't find any fault with Texas Rex promoting Dwight."

"It certainly seems like a fair decision," replied Kat.

"'Seems'?" said Wolfe. "Come on, Kat. Admit it. Dwight Knight showed real leadership. How can you possibly think he shouldn't be rewarded for jumping into an impossible situation and saving the day?"

"I'm not arguing with you Wolfe. Dwight faced a crisis and performed admirably. He took the initiative and got the job done."

Kat looked thoughtful, but said nothing more.

"Tex seemed like he was being straight with us when he said he'd have promoted Zoë without hesitation if it hadn't been for Dwight's unique feat. Did you believe him?" Wolfe asked.

"Yes, I did," said Kat.

Several moments passed.   When Wolfe could no longer take the silence, he asked, "So . . . is there anything to talk about?"

Kat finally pulled out of her reverie and smiled at Wolfe. ""No, I guess not—at least, not about Zoë.   But we do need to schedule a meeting with Bernie sometime next week to go over what we've found.

"We sure do," agreed Wolfe. "I can finish my report over the weekend. I'll set something up with Bernie for Monday. How does that sound."

"It sounds fine, Wolfe." Kat smiled. "And Wolfe—"

He looked up.

"Thank you!"

L essons for Zoë

Sometimes, life's just *like* that . . . .

REPORT TO BERNIE

Feline Foods
The finest feline feast in the East

HIGHLY CONFIDENTIAL – FOR YOUR EYES ONLY

To: Bernard Rottweiler, President & CEO
From: Ryan Wolfhound, Executive VP, Special Projects
Date: February 11, 3003
Re: Report on Kathryn Wu
Attached: Kat's Report

Issue: 1.   How can Feline Foods increase the number of 'promotable' felines?

            2.   Would hiring Kathryn Wu to train staff resolve the issue?

Conclusion: Yes.

Findings:

1.   Our four sets of interviews confirmed that canines and felines do tend to have different perceptions of how the workplace does and should function.

2.   Kat was able to identify these differences, show how they created misunderstandings between the employees and supervisors, and suggest ways to resolve these issues.

3.   Kat kept her word about not dealing in "fault" or "blame." In fact, there were times that I felt the canine supervisor was wrong in his thinking or decision. In each case, Kat identified perfectly rational and reasonable explanations for what he thought and did. Over the four days, I became convinced that it really isn't a matter of "fault" but rather exactly what Kat says it is – a totally different way of seeing things.

Conclusion

February 11, 3003   page -2-

4. The benefits I saw in Kat's approach are as follows:
- Canines will be open to listening to what Kat has to say because:
  ➢ She is NOT telling them that they are wrong.
  ➢ She is NOT telling them that they have to change.
  ➢ She IS giving them information that will enhance their ability to communicate with their feline employees (and/or bosses).
- Felines will be open to what Kat has to say because:
  ➢ She trains felines how to avoid the communication styles and patterns that give the appearance of being weak or "lacking confidence," which seems to be a problem here.
  ➢ She doesn't *insist* that felines change, but rather empowers them with tools they need if they *want* to pursue career "success" in the traditional sense. (There are some felines—and some canines—who enjoy their 'work' and don't want the stress of "pushing" their way up the career ladder. But at the same time, they don't want to feel that their contributions are overlooked or that they are the victims of discrimination. Learning all of the effort that goes into "managing" a career up that ladder lets them understand that they do have a choice.)
  ➢ She has a track record of success at Compu-Cat.

If you have any further questions, please give me a call.

Wolfe

P.S. I have reviewed and attached Kat's Report, which consists of a summary of the four interview sets and a series of "Lessons" that give you a sense of the material she covers in the training courses.

Part 6:
Conclusion

"Thus a skilled warrior subdues enemy troops without raising arms; captures cities without laying siege; destroys countries without lengthy warfare."

Found in the Historical data files, from the Ancient Year 2007 --by Chin-Ning Chu, The Art of War for Women

CANINE COMMENTS

Monday morning dawned bright and beautiful as Kat prepared herself mentally to meet with Bernie. She arrived at the Executive Suite about ten minutes early for the 10:00 a.m. meeting. Martha welcomed her warmly, gave her a steaming cup of coffee, and led her to a comfortable sofa overlooking the harbor of this major metropolis.

Kat's mind wasn't on the view, however. She was thinking about the conversation she'd had with Zoë Katz over lunch on Friday. It had been quite enlightening. She was wondering exactly how to use what Zoë had told her to make a very valuable point about leadership, when she was distracted by the voices of Wolfe and Texas Rex. They didn't notice Kat as they crossed the suite and disappeared into whatever lay behind the intricately carved mahogany doors. Kat's antenna went up. What was going on?

Just before 10, Bernie emerged from his office. He smiled broadly when he saw Kat and rang out with a booming "Good morning, Kat! How the heck are you this fine day?"

"I'm wonderful, Bernie. And yourself?"

"Great, as always!" said Bernie. "So, have you seen Wolfe's report?" he asked with what Kat thought was a twinkle in his big brown eyes.

"No, I haven't" she replied calmly.

"Well, I won't keep you in suspense. He spoke very highly of you and your work. Recommended I hire you, in fact."

"I'm glad to hear that," said Kat. She waited, but Bernie didn't offer anything further.

"We're going to meet in the Board Room this morning," said Bernie, walking Kat toward the massive doors that Wolfe and Tex had entered just moments before. "I've asked a few others to join us.

The doors opened into a large, well-appointed conference room. Kat recognized everyone seated around the opulent oval conference table. At the far end on the left sat Hyrum N. Fyrum, the canine who'd introduced her to Feline Foods. To Hyrum's right, in the center seat, sat Oliver Wendell Hounds. Princeton Pointer sat in the seat nearest to Kat on the left. To her right, the line-up was Wolfe, in the seat farthest from her, Texas Rex in the middle, and Ashford Huntington, III in the near seat.

As Kat sized up the room and its occupants, Bernie walked to the far end of the table and took the seat at its head. He motioned for her to be seated in the remaining chair, opposite him at the foot of the table.

The canines were looking at her with interest, but she sensed no hostility. Nonetheless, the environment was a bit intimidating, even for Kat. She assumed a professional smile, nodded politely toward each side of the table in turn, and said,

"Good morning, gentledogs." Then she sat down. This was Bernie's show.

"Kat," he began, "Let me begin by telling you that I'm impressed with you and your work and I'm inclined to offer you a contract. The fact that you were able to win Wolfe's confidence is nothing short of miraculous!" There were a few chuckles around the room at Wolfe's expense.

"But before we finalize the deal, I wanted to give these canines an opportunity to ask any question they had about the interviews. If I decide to use your services, I don't want any lingering concerns floating around among my executives. You don't mind, do you?"

Bernie didn't really expect an answer and Kat didn't offer one. She raised her eyebrows expectantly.

"Just so you'll know," continued Bernie, "everyone in this room—and ONLY the canines in the room—are aware of who you interviewed. So if it's necessary to discuss specifics, you can do so without revealing anything they don't already know." Bernie looked down the table, to his left.

"Pointer," said Bernie, "let's start with you."

Princeton Pointer turned to Kat and, without preface, began.

"I want to know what your intentions are, Ms. Kat. I want to know if you intend to force me to promote felines like . . . well, let's not deal in personalities, here. You say that's not your intent, but I felt *very* uncomfortable in that interview. I felt you were clearly challenging my decisions."

Kat took a moment to gather her thought.

"First, thank you for speaking frankly. I mean that," she added quickly, seeing skepticism in his eyes. "I also need to thank you—to thank all of you—for speaking frankly during our interviews. Let me assure you that if Wolfe and I seemed to be challenging you, it was only to be sure we were getting the truth—which I believe we did, from each of you."

Kat turned back to Princeton.

"Let me ask you something. If it hadn't been for the "memo" incident, would you have wanted to promote Ms. Lyons?"

"Of course I would," replied Princeton. "I hired her because she showed promise. "

"And it takes time and money to hire and train a new employee, right?"

"Yes, it does!"

"It has to be not only costly, but frustrating to have a promising employee disappoint you."

"*Very* frustrating," said Princeton. "But I *can*not promote someone who ignores hierarchy—who violates the *cardinal* rule of the workplace."

"Because in your experience, *everyone* in the workplace knows the 'cardinal rule,' right? And anyone who deliberately violates it is disloyal and can't be trusted?"

"Precisely," agreed Princeton.

"But what if I told you that most felines *don't* perceive loyalty to the hierarchy as absolute?"

"I'd say that there's *no excuse* for undermining your superiors!"

"What about loyalty to the Company, Princeton? That's where most felines place their loyalty and that's why Kitty Lyons wrote that memo. She was trying to protect Feline Foods!"

"But she did it the *wrong way!*" Princeton growled.

"Yes, she did," said Kat, immediately calming Pointer. "And a major purpose of my training is to teach felines these ;unwritten' rules of the workplace—all of the 'right' ways of doing things, of interacting, of communicating—that canines have developed and learned to do instinctively over the centuries they've ruled the workplace."

Princeton drew in a long breath as he contemplated what Kat said. After a moment or two, Bernie spoke up.

"Does that satisfy you, Princeton?"

"I suppose so," replied Princeton. "As long as she's not making this problem *my* fault."

"That's MY cardinal rule, Princeton. I don't find *blame;* I find *solutions.*"

Bernie turned his gaze to the far end of the table and found Ashford Huntington, III. "Ashford," he bellowed jovially. "Any questions for Kat?"

Ashford shook the long silky fur back from his face and smiled warmly at Kat. "I think she'll do a wonderful job," he said, drawing moans and mutters of 'suck-up' from several of his fellow canines.

Ignoring them all, he continued. "I do have a question, Kat. After we talked, I realized that I could have been more direct with the feline we discussed. But I didn't know how to say what needed to be said. Does your course include training to help supervisors effectively communicate difficult topics and negative evaluations?"

"Now *there's* a softball!" grinned Bernie.

Kat turned to Ashford to respond. "Actually, Ashford, I have a series of courses to help supervisors with evaluation skills. Most of them deal with exactly what you asked about—how to say the difficult things. Other aspects of the training are learning to give *immediate* feedback and knowing *what* feedback needs to be given."

Seeing that Ashford was satisfied, Bernie turned back to the canines sitting around the table. "Oliver—your turn."

Oliver sat up, slowly, choosing his words carefully, as always.

"Perhaps I'm just the proverbial 'old dog', Bernie, but I just don't see what Ms. Wu could possibly do that would make any difference in the situation with the feline she and I discussed."

Bernie turned to Kat. "There's a challenge for you, Kat. How do you respond to Oliver?"

Kat realized that she couldn't go into all of the details about communication that she and Wolfe had discussed. But maybe she could make at least one point.

Turning to Bernie, she said, "You're sure it's okay to talk specifics?"

"Looks to me like Oliver's question requires it," replied Bernie.

"Okay, then, Oliver. Let's talk about the Sandbox case for a minute."

"I've said all there is to say about that case. My feline attorney wasn't able to negotiate a decent settlement. There was no excuse for offering one penny more than $2 million! Now we have to go to trial. Period. End of discussion."

Kat took a deep breath. "Oliver, did you know that Buddy Bassett had over two million dollars in *medical bills*?"

Oliver looked startled. "No, I didn't. But that really has nothing to do with the negotiations . . ."

"Of course it does," replied Kat rather sharply. "Did you know that Buddy was keenly aware that the first $2 million of any settlement would be paid by Feline Foods' *insurance* company, rather than the company itself?"

"Well, no, but what the . . ."

Kat kept going. "Did you know that Buddy Bassett was furious with Feline Foods *before* the accident because they were making him retire? That he wanted to make the *company* PAY in this case? That $2 million wasn't a negotiation amount; it was a *base?!*"

Oliver was turning red and sputtering. "Well, why . . . I mean . . ."

Kat finished the point. "And if you *had* known all this, it would have made a huge difference in your decision about settling the case, wouldn't it?"

Oliver was beside himself. "Well of COURSE it would have! But why DIDN'T I know? Let me ask you that. Why didn't Havana TELL ME?! This doesn't help your case. This is just another example of Havana's incompetence!"

Kat responded immediately. "Not *another* example, Oliver, a *different* concern. "

Oliver looked puzzled.

Kat explained. "When you didn't know all the facts, you were critical of Havana's negotiating skills. You felt she didn't push hard enough. And you concluded that because she 'left money on the table' you couldn't trust her work. Isn't that more or less what you told us?"

"Well, yes," said Oliver. "And my conclusions were perfectly legitimate, under the circumstances!"

"No doubt," replied Kat. "But now that you have all of the facts, wouldn't you agree that Havana's negotiating strategy was right on target?"

Oliver looked wary. "Well, assuming what you've told me is true, I suppose there was no possibility of settling the case for much less than $4 million. But that doesn't excuse Havana's failure to keep me advised of these facts!"

"I agree," said Kat. "But let me ask you this. How much information do you generally *want* from your attorneys?"

"I want enough so that I can have confidence in how they're handling their cases," replied Oliver.

"And how will they *know* how much is enough? For example, how would Havana know that you questioned her settlement strategy? She came to you for approval of the $4 million settlement amount and you gave it. Did you ask for her strategy at that point?"

"Well, no ... but ..."

"But you had some doubts, at that point, right? That's when you asked Cocky Spaniel to get involved in the case . . . to give you some feedback on how things were going?"

"So, you're saying the outcome is MY fault because I didn't *solicit* adequate information from Ms. Brown?" Oliver gave Bernie a meaningful glance then said to Kat. "So much for the claim that you don't blame canines!"

Kat took a deep breath. This was a make or break moment for her.

"But I'm *not* blaming you, Oliver. I'm just making the point that the entire issue between you and Havana was caused by a 'failure to communicate.' Havana doesn't understand the pressure you, or any boss, is under, being totally responsible for the work that others are actually doing. It just doesn't occur to her that no matter how much confidence you may have in any member of your staff, there are times, particularly when the stakes are high, that you need to be reassured that they're on the right track. Havana is very direct. She has a lot of confidence in her own abilities and assumes that you have confidence in her *unless you tell her otherwise.*

"Much calmer now, Oliver noted, "Yes, that's all very true."

Kat continued, "You on the other hand, Oliver, communicate more indirectly. You assume your employees are in the best position to determine what you may need to know. In this case, Havana's expectations of directness ran afoul of your indirect communication."

"But what is your *point?*" asked Oliver.

"Simply this, Oliver," said Kat. "You asked what can I possibly offer that would have helped your situation with Havana? My entire training program is focused on promoting effective communication between canines and felines."

"I see," mused Oliver, gently rubbing his paw across his forehead. "So you would be teaching me new ways to communicate with my attorneys?" asked Oliver.

"No!" said Wolfe, from the opposite end of the table.

All eyes turned at this unexpected interruption.

"Sorry," said Wolfe, grinning sheepishly. "Kat and I had this exact conversation. It just slipped out."

Kat smiled, pleased that Wolfe had inadvertently bolstered her credibility.

"Wolfe is right, Oliver. I don't ask the 'boss' to change. You have too many direct reports to worry about how to talk to each one. I train subordinates how to be much more sensitive to the informational needs of their bosses. They learn to find out how much information you need, what kind of information you like to have, when you need it, and the form in which you prefer to get information—written or verbal."

"That sounds pretty darn good!" offered Texas Rex, who was tired of sitting and listening. "That okay with you, Ollie?"

Oliver winced at Tex's use of the diminutive form of his name, but responded with a grudging, "I suppose so."

"Great!" said Texas. "I guess it's my turn."

WHY MUST THERE BE DRAGONS?

Without waiting for Bernie's affirmation, Texas launched into his comments, with his Texas drawl in high gear, "Ah don't have any objectshun to us hiring Ms. Wu, Bernie. 'Course ah didn't have any of these same probl'ms with my felines. Nope, there was no question that promotin' Dwight Knight was the best decision, right, Ms. Kat?"

Before Kat could answer, Bernie added his thoughts on Dwight's achievements.

"Now there's the epitome of a leader. Did you meet Dwight Knight, Kat?" Without waiting for a response, Bernie continued. "That young pup single-handedly saved this Company not only several million dollars, but a ton of embarrassment!"

"So I heard," she responded, "Texas Rex entertained us with a full account of Dwight's efforts."

"Dwight Knight is this Company's 'White Knight'" said Tex, grinning at the play on words . . . "he's a real dragon-slayer. Ms. Woo. With all due respect—and believe me, I <u>do</u> respect cats. I know the work they're capable of doing. But I have to say that in all my years in business, I've just never seen a cat show that kind of take-charge leadership. Dwight's the kind of leader who rises to the challenge of a dragon-sized crisis and cuts off its head!"

A subtle gleam appeared in Kat's deep blue eyes. "Suppose I were to show you that one of your felines exerted a brand of leadership far *superior* to Mr. Knight's with respect to the very same issue."

"That's impossible!" said Tex dismissively.. "No one else had to deal with *Regulation G* like Dwight did."

"Ah," said Kat, "but suppose I can prove what I just said? What would that be worth to you?"

Tex broke into a broad grin; he loved a challenge. "Hell, little feline, you prove that and I'll not only tell Bernie to hire you but to take your fee right out of my budget! Heh, heh, heh."

Kat smiled and looked to Wolfe, who got up and walked out of the conference room.

"Bernie, I've asked Zoë Katz to join us, if you don't mind. Wolfe has gone to get her."

"Zoë Katz?" said Bernie, "Isn't she Vice President of Economy Brands Sales & Marketing? I thought *Regulation G* only applied to Premium cat food?"

"You're half right," replied Kat. "Only Premium cat food has to have the new vitamin, Kormien, in it. But *Regulation G* requires a label about Kormien to be on ALL brands and qualities of cat food."

"Well, there weren't any delivery problems with our economy brands," said Tex. "At least, nothin' I heard about!"

"That's true—" Kat stopped in mid-sentence, as Wolfe returned to the conference room with Zoë.

While Wolfe procured an extra chair for the newcomer, Zoë greeted the canines around the table.

Pleasantries completed, Kat took over.

"Zoë, I've asked you to come in to talk about your division's experience with the new *Regulation G*."

"What do you want to know?" asked Zoë, aware of the problems in the Premium division, but uncertain how that related to what Kat was asking.

Kat answered her. "When you and I had lunch, on Friday, you told me that the Economy Brand division recently delivered $13 million worth of Tabby Treats to the restaurant unit of Heartbreak Hotels."

"They took delivery Thursday, a week ago," said Zoë.

"And did the Tabby Treats packaging have the new label on it? The one required by *Regulation G*?" asked Kat.

"Yes," said Zoë, simply, deciding to let Kat draw the story out of her rather than seeming too eager.

Tex jumped in, his anger beginning to foment. "Wait a durn minute. This makes no sense. I was told that Regs&Legs didn't notify *any* of the operating divisions about *Regulation G*. Somebody around here been givin' me wrong information?"

"Not at all, Texas," Zoë responded. "No one got notified. I just recently found out what happened. R&L did send out a timely email notice about *Regulation G*, but unfortunately, it was one of the few that got lost in the Internet ether-world during the company's year-end transition to the new system."

"Then how did you know about it?" Tex asked suspiciously.

Kat jumped in before Zoë could answer, wanting to tell this part of the story in her own way.

"I'll tell you how, Texas. Before *any* order over $1 million is finalized for delivery in Zoë's department, her staff goes through a checklist to be sure that all of the details have been taken care of. Zoë implemented this system shortly after she took over the division. And no, the Sales & Marketing staff does not do the work of the other departments. Zoë trusts that everyone in the Company does their job. In the words of one of our former Presidents, however, you should 'trust, but verify.' Before the Heartbreak Hotel order could be finalized, Zoë's staff performed its customary checks, and when they called R&L, they learned about *Regulation G.*"

"Just in time," added Zoë. "We actually had to postpone the delivery for three days in order to get the labels added to the packaging."

Texas Rex was on his feet, pacing back and forth, obviously disturbed. "So, why didn't you notify Dwight's department about this *Regulation G* requirement?"

Zoë paused, and looked over at Kat before replying. "Actually, I did," she said, finally.

Tex looked up sharply. "You told Dwight about this? When did you talk with him?"

"I didn't talk directly with Dwight. He was out when I called. I spoke with his administrative assistant, Snoopy. That was on the 9th—the day I learned of the problem."

"That's the day before Dwight's big shipment went out," said Kat. "Dwight probably didn't get the message in time," said

Kat, who could see that Tex was fuming and was seeking a target for his anger. That was not Kat's goal.

Kat waited for Tex to focus on her before continuing. "Look, Texas, I'm not in any way saying that Dwight didn't do a great job, under the circumstances. He provided one kind of leadership – crisis leadership. And he did it well.

"What I *am* saying is that Zoë provided another kind of leadership—crisis-avoidance.

"Dwight may have risen to the challenge and slain the dragon who was threatening the Company village. . . But Zoë never let the dragon anywhere near the village. Indeed, you never even knew there was a dragon threatening the economy brand."

"That, Mr. Rex, is the *best* kind of leadership! Real leaders *prevent* crises—they never let the dragon get anywhere near the village, much less, in the door. The question you to might want to ask the next time is why must there *be* dragons?"

> "The art of war is to win without fighting."
>
> Found in the Historical Files, from Ancient Year 2007
> Chin-Ning Chu, The Art of War for Women

Appendices

S ELECTED REFERENCES & RECOMMENDED READINGS IN THE HISTORICAL FILES FROM THE ANCIENT YEARS

Binchy, Maeve, "King's Cross," from *London Transports*, Dell Publishing, 1995

Chu, Chin-ning, *The Art of War for Women: Sun Tzu's Ancient Strategies and Wisdom for Winning at Work*, 2007

Evans, Gail, *Play Like A Man, Win Like A Woman: What Men Know About Success that Women Need to Learn*, Broadway Books, 2000

Fiorina, Carly, *Tough Choices*, Penguin Group, 2006

Foley, Mary, *bodacious! Career: Outrageous Success for Working Women*, Bodacious Books, 2004

Frankel, Lois P., *Nice Girls Don't Get the Corner Office: 101 Unconscious Mistakes Women Make that Sabotage Their Careers*, Warner Business Books, 2004

Frankel, Lois P., *See Jane Lead: 99 Ways for Women to Take Charge at Work*, Warner Business Books, 2007

Gilligan, Carol, *In A Different Voice: Psychological Theory and Women's Development*, Harvard University Press, 1982, 1993

Grey, John, *Mars and Venus in the Workplace*, Harper Collins, 2002

Harragan, Betty Lehan, *Games Mother Never Taught You: Corporate Gamesmanship for Women*, Warner Books, 1977

Heim, Pat & Golant, Susan K. *Smashing the Glass* Ceiling, Fireside, 1995 (formerly, Hardball *for Women: Winning at the Game of Business*, Plume, 1993)

Helgesen, Sally, *The Female Advantage: Women's Ways of Leadership*, Currency Doubleday, 1990, 1995

Klaus, Peggy, *Brag! The Art of Tooting Your Own Horn Without Blowing It*, Warner Books, 2003

Mendell, Adrienne, *How Men Think: The Seven Essential Rules for Making it in a Man's World*, Ballentine Books, 1996

Mindell, Phyllis, *A Woman's Guide to the Language of Success: Communicating with Confidence and Power*, Prentice Hall, 1995

Mindell, Phyllis, *How to Say it for Women: Communicating with Confidence and Power Using the Language of Success*, Prentice Hall Press 2001

Molloy, John T., *The Woman's Dress for Success Book*, Warner Books, 1980

O'Brian, Virginia, *Success on Our Own Terms: Tales of Extraordinary, Ordinary Business Women*, John Wiley & Sons, Inc. 1998

Tannen, Deborah, *Talking from 9 to 5: How Women's and Men's Conversational Sytles Affect Who Gets Heard, Who Gets Credit, and What Gets Done at Work*, 1994

Trunk, Penelope, *Brazen Careerist: The* New *Rules for Success*, Warner Business Books, 2007

White, Kate, *Why Good Girls Don't Get Ahead. . .But Gutsy Girls Do: 9 Secrets Every Working Woman Must Know*, Warner Books, 2002

Congratulations!

You've finished this book, and now qualify to own and proudly wear a "Bi-Lingual DOG" or a "Bi-Lingual CAT" tee shirt.

To get your tee shirt, go online to www.GenderStrategy.com or complete the Order Form on the following page.

ORDER FORM

Please send me the following:

Quantity	Item	Price Each	Total Price
☐	Bi-Lingual DOG tee shirt(s)	$10.00	_____
☐	Bi-Lingual CAT tee shirt(s)	$10.00	_____
☐	Additional Copies of this Book	$14.95	_____
	Shipping & Handling		$2.95
	Sales Tax (Maryland residents add 6%)		_____
	TOTAL AMOUNT ENCLOSED (Check or Money Order)		_____

Ship to:
Name: _____

Address:_____

Phone: _____ **Email:** _____
(for confirmation purposes)

Send check or money order for the Total Amount along with the Order Form to:

GenderStrategy
3104 Fox Valley Drive
Suite 100
West Friendship, MD 21794

Allow two weeks for delivery.

www.GenderStrategy.com

176

Made in the USA